ROTARY WING

An edited reprint of selected portions of the

U.S. Army Field Manual 1-51

Compiled and edited by

Nicholas Ean

INTRODUCTION

ROTARY WING FLIGHT

The following document has been edited and reprinted as a helicopter primary training manual and reference text, deleting the sections of the Army manual FM 1-51 that do not apply to **primary** flight training.

TABLE OF CONTENTS

CHAPTER 1

GLOSSARY

acceleration—The rate of change of velocity with respect to time.

advancing blade—The rotor blade experiencing an increased relative wind because of airspeed.

airfoil—A surfaced body designed to produce a force when subjected to an airflow.

airfoil section—A cross section of an airfoil.

airspeed—The speed of an aircraft in relation to the air. It is a component of relative wind.

altitude—The elevation of an aircraft above a given reference plane.

angle of attack—The acute angle between the chord line of an airfoil and the resultant relative wind.

angle of incidence (Also called pitch angle.)—The angle of the rotor blade chord line with the plane of rotation (tip-path plane) of the rotor system.

antitorque—A method used to counteract the torque reaction which results from turning the rotor system.

articulated rotor system—A rotor system in which the hub is mounted rigidly to the mast, and the individual blades are mounted on hinge pins, allowing them to flap up and down and move forward and backward. Individual blades are allowed to feather by rotating about the blade grip retainer bearing.

autorotation—The action of turning a rotor system by airflow and not by engine power. The airflow may be produced by forward movement or descending through the air.

axis—The theoretical line extending through the center of gravity of an aircraft in each major plane.

axis of rotation—The center of rotation perpendicular to the plane of rotation.

bank—To roll about the longitudinal axis of the aircraft.

blow back—The tendency for the rotor disk to tilt aft as a result of flapping that is caused by the combined effects of dissymmetry of lift and transverse flow.

camber—The curvature of an airfoil.

center of gravity—The point within an aircraft through which, for balance purposes, the total force of gravity is considered to act.

center of pressure—A point along the chord line of an airfoil through which all the aerodynamic forces are considered to act.

centrifugal force—A force that tends to make rotating bodies move away from the center of rotation.

centripetal force—A force that counteracts centrifugal force by keeping a system a certain radius from the axis of rotation.

chord—The longitudinal dimension of an airfoil section, measured from the leading to trailing edge.

induced velocity (V_i)—The induced vertical component of the relative wind, sometimes referred to as "downwash."

rotational velocity (V_r)—The component of the relative wind produced by rotation of the rotor blades.

retreating blade—The rotor blade experiencing a decreased relative wind because of airspeed.

retreating blade stall—A stall that begins at or near the tip of the blade due to high angles of attack required to compensate for dissymmetry of lift.

rigid rotor system—A rotor system in which the rotor blades are fixed rigidly to the hub and not allowed to flap or lead and lag. The only action allowed is pitch change.

roll—Movement about the longitudinal axis.

semirigid rotor system—A rotor system in which the blades are connected to the mast by a trunnion that allows blades to flap. Pitch change (feathering) is allowed at the hub about the blade grip retainer bearing.

settling with power—A condition of powered flight where the helicopter settles in its own downwash.

skid—Rate of turn is greater than normal for the degree of bank established.

slip—Rate of turn is less than normal for the degree of bank established.

slug—The unit of mass that is accelerated at the rate of 1 foot per second when acted upon by a force of 1 pound weight.

speed—The rate at which an object moves.

stall—A condition of an airfoil at which it is at an angle of attack greater than the angle of attack of maximum lift.

tail rotor—The antitorque device of a single-rotor helicopter. Control of this rotor is through the foot pedals.

tandem rotor system—A main lifting rotor is used at each end of the helicopter. The rotor systems rotate in opposite direction to counteract torque.

thrust—The force which opposes drag. In rotary-wing aircraft, often expressed as the total lift of the rotor system (T_r).

tip-path plane—A plane defined by the circle scribed by the average flightpath of the blade tips in a rotor system. It is sometimes called the rotor disk.

torque effect—The reaction to the turning of the rotor system. If the rotor system turns counterclockwise, the fuselage reacts by turning clockwise. (See Newton's third law.)

total aerodynamic force—The total force developed by an airfoil (lift + drag).

translational flight—Any horizontal movement of the helicopter with respect to the air.

translational lift—Additional lift obtained because of airspeed.

translating tendency—The tendency of the single-rotor helicopter to move laterally during hovering flight (also called tail rotor drift).

transverse flow effect—A condition of increased drag in the aft portion of the rotor disk caused by the air having a greater downwash angle in the aft portion of the disk.

vector—A quantity having both magnitude and direction. Also a graphic illustration of such a quantity.

velocity—A vector quantity having both speed and direction.

weight—A measure of the mass of an object under the acceleration of gravity.

work—A force exerted over a given distance.

yaw—Movement about the vertical axis.

chord line—A straight line connecting the leading and trailing edges of an airfoil.

coefficient of drag (C_D)—A dimensionless number indicating the drag inefficiency of an airfoil which is determined by angle of attack and airfoil design. It is derived from wind tunnel testing.

coefficient of lift (C_L)—A dimensionless number indicating the efficiency of the airfoil which is determined by angle of attack and airfoil design. It is derived from wind tunnel testing.

collective feathering—The simultaneous change of pitch of all rotor blades in a rotor system an equal amount.

compressibility effects—A phenomenon resulting from the advancing blade approaching Mach I or the speed of sound, due to excessive forward speed. As the blade reaches the critical Mach number, a shock wave is formed. This shock wave changes the density of the air and causes separation of the airflow rearward of the shock wave. The most adverse effect is a shift of center of pressure from the first third of the chord position causing a severe twisting moment on the blade.

coning angle—The angle between the plane of rotation and the rotor blade.

cyclic feathering—The change of pitch of individual rotor blades independently of the other blades in the system.

dissymmetry of lift—The difference in lift exists between the advancing half of the rotor disk and the retreating half.

drag (D)—A force opposing the motion of a body through the air.

flapping—Up and down movement of a rotor blade.

friction—A force which opposes motion.

gravity—An attraction of two objects for each other that is dependent upon their mass and the distance between them.

ground effect—A condition of improved aircraft performance when operating near a surface.

gyroscopic precession—A phenomenon in rotating systems that makes all forces react with a movement 90° from the point of force in the direction of rotation.

induced drag (D_i)—Airfoil drag induced by the production of aerodynamic force.

kinetic energy—The energy of a system because of motion.

lead and lag—Movement of the rotor blade forward (lead) and aft (lag) of the radial line from the center of the main rotor shaft through the axis of the drag hinge.

lift (L)—The net force developed perpendicular to the relative wind.

mass—The amount of material in a body normally expressed in slugs.

mean camber line—A line drawn halfway between the upper and lower surfaces of an airfoil. On symmetrical airfoils, the mean camber line and the chord line are the same.

parasite drag (D_p)—Drag incurred from the nonlifting portions of the aircraft includes all form and skin friction drag.

pitch (attitude)—Movement about the lateral axis.

potential energy—The energy of a system derived from position.

power—The rate of doing work, often expressed in units of horsepower.

profile drag (D_o)—The parasite drag of the helicopter rotor blades.

relative wind (V)—The airflow relative to an airfoil.

airspeed velocity (V_a)—The component of the relative wind produced by forward movement of the aircraft.

flapping velocity (V_f)—The component of the relative wind produced by blade flapping.

CHAPTER 2

HELICOPTER AERODYNAMICS

FLIGHT THEORY

Helicopter flight theory is based on the laws of motion and pressure differential that govern the flight of all conventional heavier-than-air craft. Aviators should understand these laws in order to more easily master the helicopter aerodynamics that follow. A description of vector and scalar quantities is also included, and provides a vehicle to simplify the explanation of aerodynamics.

CONTENTS

NEWTON'S LAWS OF MOTION

Newton's three laws of motion are *inertia, acceleration,* and *action-reaction.* These laws are applicable to the flight of rotary-wing. Knowledge of the laws of motion will help aviators to understand the rotary-wing aerodynamics discussed in later sections of this chapter.

☐ The first law, *inertia,* states that a body at rest will remain at rest, and a body in motion will remain in motion at the same speed and in the same direction until affected by some external force. Nothing starts or stops without an outside force to bring about or prevent motion. Hence, the force with which a body offers resistance to change is called the force of inertia.

☐ The second law, *acceleration,* asserts that the force required to produce a change in motion of a body is directly proportional to its *mass* and the *rate of change* in its velocity. Acceleration may be due to an increase or a decrease in velocity, although deceleration is commonly used to indicate a decrease.

☐ The third law, *action-reaction,* states that for every action there is an equal and opposite reaction. If an interaction occurs between two bodies, equal forces in opposite directions will be imparted to each body.

BERNOULLI'S PRINCIPLE

Daniel Bernoulli, one of a family of Swiss mathematicians, stated a principle that describes the relationship between internal fluid pressure and fluid velocity. His principle, essentially a statement of the conservation of energy, explains at least in part why an airfoil develops an aerodynamic force.

All of the forces acting on a surface over which there is a flow of air are the result of *pressure* or *skin friction.* Friction forces are the result of viscosity and are confined to a very thin layer of air near the surface. They usually are not dominant, and from the pilot's perspective can be discounted with concentration instead on pressure distribution.

As an aid in visualizing what happens to pressure as air flows over an airfoil, it is helpful to consider flow through a tube (fig 2-1). The concept of conservation of mass states that mass cannot be created or destroyed; so what goes in one end of a tube must come out the other end. If the flow through a tube is neither accelerating nor decelerating at the input, then the mass of flow per unit of time at station 1 must equal the mass of flow per unit of time at station 2 and so on through station 3. The mass of flow per unit of time is called the *mass flow rate* and may be computed from the following equation:

Mass Flow Rate $= \rho A V$

Where: ρ (rho) = previously defined density.

A = Area of the section through which the flow is proceeding.

V = Velocity of the flow at the section in question.

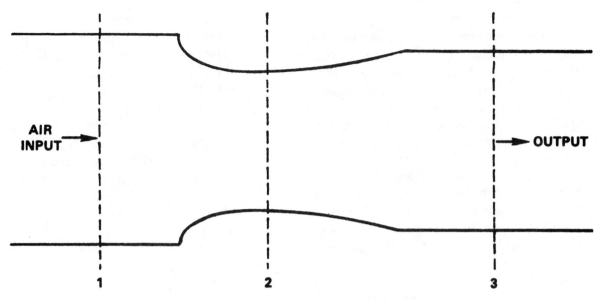

FIGURE 2-1. FLOW THROUGH A TUBE.

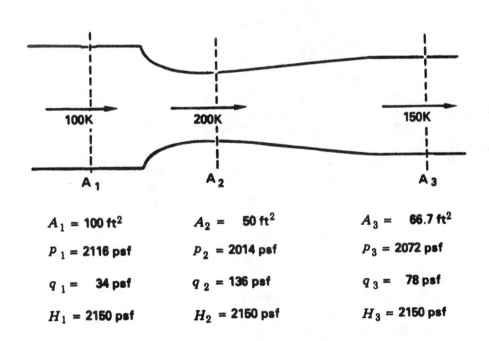

$A_1 = 100 \text{ ft}^2$	$A_2 = 50 \text{ ft}^2$	$A_3 = 66.7 \text{ ft}^2$
$p_1 = 2116 \text{ psf}$	$p_2 = 2014 \text{ psf}$	$p_3 = 2072 \text{ psf}$
$q_1 = 34 \text{ psf}$	$q_2 = 136 \text{ psf}$	$q_3 = 78 \text{ psf}$
$H_1 = 2150 \text{ psf}$	$H_2 = 2150 \text{ psf}$	$H_3 = 2150 \text{ psf}$

FIGURE 2-2. CHANGES OF PRESSURE AND VELOCITY WITH AREA.

The mass flow equation may be simplified in the low subsonic range because changes in density are so slight they can be neglected in all but the most precise calculations. At low flight speeds, air experiences relatively small changes in pressure and negligible changes in density. This airflow is termed incompressible, since the air may undergo changes in pressure without apparent changes in density. Such a condition of airflow is analogous to the flow of water, hydraulic fluid, or any other incompressible fluid. Thus, an equation may be written describing the flow through the stations in figure 2-1 as follows:

$$A_1 V_1 = A_2 V_2 = A_3 V_3$$

This equation suggests that between any two points in the tube, the velocity varies inversely with the area. Thus, if A_1 is greater than A_2 (as it is in fig 2-1), V_2 must be greater than V_1. Venturi effect is the name used to describe this phenomena. Fluid flow speeds up through the restricted area of a venturi in direct proportion to the reduction in area. Figure 2-2 suggests what happens to the speed of the flow through the tube. A discussion of compressible flow and its effects is included in a later paragraph.

Total energy in a given closed system does not change, but the form of the energy may be altered. Pressure of flowing air may be likened to energy in that the total pressure of flowing air will always remain constant unless energy is added or taken from the flow. In the example in figures 2-1 and 2-2, there is no addition or subtraction of energy, so total pressure will remain constant.

Fluid flow pressure is made up of two components, static pressure, and dynamic pressure. The static pressure is the pressure that would be measured by an aneroid placed in the flow, but not moving with the flow as it measured the pressure. The dynamic pressure of the flow is that component of total pressure that is due to the motion of the air. It is difficult to measure directly, but a pitot static tube measures it indirectly. The sum of these two pressures is total pressure and is measured by allowing the flow to impact against an open end tube which is vented to an aneroid. The equation describing the sum of these pressures is written as follows:

$$H = p + q$$

where: H = total pressure

p = static pressure

q = dynamic pressure

q = $\frac{1}{2} \rho V^2$

The equation shown above is the incompressible or slow speed form of the Bernoulli equation. Written about the flow in figure 2-1, it would be the following:

$$H_1 = H_2 = H_3$$

or

$$p_1 + \tfrac{1}{2} \rho V_1^2 = p_2 + \tfrac{1}{2} \rho V_2^2 = p_3 + \tfrac{1}{2} \rho V_3^2$$

Variations of pressure and velocity with area may be seen in figure 2-2. Note that static pressure decreases as the velocity increases. Consider only the bottom half of a venturi tube as shown in figure 2-3. Notice how the shape of the restricted area at A_2 resembles the top surface of an airfoil. Even when the top half of the venturi tube is taken away, the air still accelerates over the curved shape of the bottom half. This is true because the air layers above act to restrict the flow just as did the top half of the venturi tube. As a result, acceleration causes decreased static pressure above the curved shape of the tube. A pressure differential force is generated by the local variation of static and dynamic pressures on the curved surface.

VECTOR AND SCALAR QUANTITIES

A study of helicopter flight is further enhanced by understanding two types of quantities, scalars and vectors. Scalar quantities are those that can be described by *size alone* such as area, volume, time, and mass. Vector quantities are those that must be described using their *size* and *direction*. Velocity, acceleration, weight, lift and drag are all common examples of vector quantities. The direction of vector quantities is just as important as the size or magnitude.

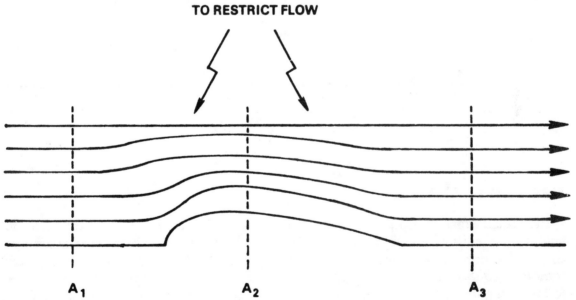

UPPER AIR LAYERS ACT

TO RESTRICT FLOW

A_1 A_2 A_3

FIGURE 2-3. VENTURI FLOW.

2-5

All forces, from whatever source, are vectors. When an object is being acted upon by two or more forces, the combined effect of these forces may be represented by the use of vectors. Vectors are graphically represented by a directed line segment with an arrow at the end. The arrow indicates the direction in which the force is acting. Line segment length in relation to a given scale represents the magnitude of the force. The vector is drawn in relation to a reference line. Magnitude is drawn to whatever scale is most convenient to the specific problem (fig 2-4).

parallel to these vectors to determine the resultant mean. When two tugboats are pushing a barge with equal force, the barge will move forward in a direction that is a mean to the direction of both tugboats (fig 2-5).

☐ *Polygon Vector Solution*. When more than two forces are acting in different directions, the resultant may be found by using a polygon vector solution. In the solution shown in figure 2-6, one force is acting at 090° with a force of 180 pounds;

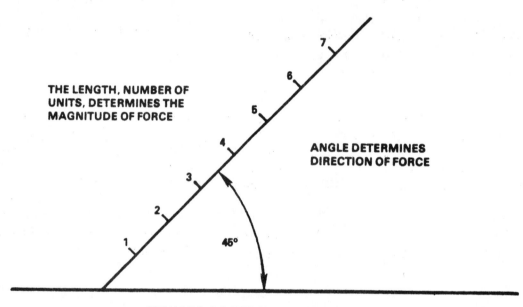

THE LENGTH, NUMBER OF UNITS, DETERMINES THE MAGNITUDE OF FORCE

ANGLE DETERMINES DIRECTION OF FORCE

45°

FIGURE 2-4. VECTOR DIAGRAM.

VECTOR SOLUTIONS

Individual force vectors are useful in analyzing conditions of flight. In the air, the chief concern is with the resultant, or combined effects, of the several component forces acting on an aircraft. Three methods of solving for resultants are:

☐ *Parallelogram*. A parallelogram contains two vectors, and lines are drawn

second force is acting at 045° with a force of 90 pounds; the third force is acting at an angle of 315° with a force of 120 pounds. To determine the resultant, draw the first vector from a point beginning at 0 (fig 2-6) and follow it with the remaining vectors, consecutively. The resultant is drawn from the point of start (0) to the ending of the final vector (C).

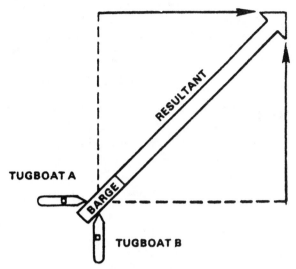

FIGURE 2-5. RESULTANT BY PARALLELOGRAM.

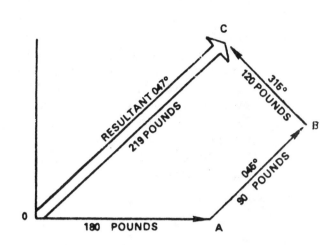

FIGURE 2-6. RESULTANT BY POLYGON.

☐ *Triangle of Vectors.* A triangle of vectors is a simplified and special form of a polygon vector solution which involves only two vectors and their resultant. It is the most commonly used vector solution in navigating.

To form a triangle of vectors, draw two vectors and connect them with a resultant line of vector. In this way, calculations may be made for drift and groundspeed. In figure 2-7, an aircraft is heading 078° with a true airspeed of 100 knots. Wind direction is from the northeast at 30 knots. By drawing a vector for each of these known velocities and drawing a connecting line between the ends, a resultant velocity is determined.

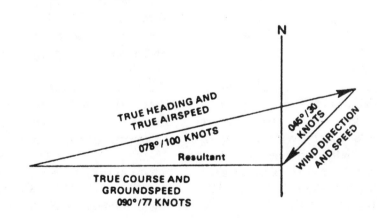

FIGURE 2-7. RESULTANT BY TRIANGULATION.

AIRFOILS

A helicopter flies for the same basic reason that any conventional heavier-than-air craft flies, because aerodynamic forces necessary to keep it aloft are produced when air passes about the rotor blades. The rotor blade, or airfoil, is the structure that makes flight possible. It is a surfaced body that produces a useful dynamic action, lift, when it passes through the air. Helicopter blades have airfoil sections designed for a specific set of flight characteristics. Some airfoil designs are less efficient under specific conditions, yet permit higher airspeeds. Other combinations of upper and lower surface designs may generate more lift, but may have a very wide center of pressure travel. Usually the designer must compromise to obtain an airfoil section that has the best flight characteristics for the mission the aircraft will perform.

Airfoil sections are of two basic types, *symmetrical* and *nonsymmetrical*. Symmetrical airfoils (fig 2-8) have identical upper and lower surfaces. They are suited to rotary-wing applications because they have almost no center of pressure travel. Travel remains relatively constant under varying angles of attack, affording the best lift-drag ratios for the full range of velocities from rotor blade root to tip. However, the symmetrical airfoil produces less lift than a nonsymmetrical airfoil and also has relatively undersirable stall characteristics. The helicopter blade (airfoil) must adapt to a wide range of airspeeds and angles of attack during each revolution of the rotor. The symmetrical airfoil delivers acceptable performance under those alternating conditions. Other benefits are lower cost and ease of construction as compared to the nonsymmetrical airfoil.

Nonsymmetrical (cambered) airfoils (fig 2-9) may have a wide variety of upper and lower surface designs. They are currently used on some CH-47 and all OH-58 Army helicopters, and are increasingly being used on newly designed aircraft. Advantages of the nonsymmetrical airfoil are increased lift-drag ratios and more desirable stall characteristics. Nonsymmetrical airfoils

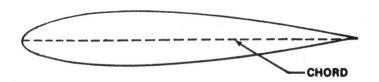

FIGURE 2-8. SYMMETRICAL AIRFOIL SECTION.

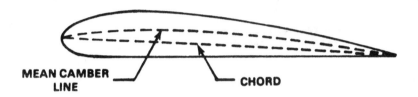

FIGURE 2-9. NONSYMMETRICAL AIRFOIL SECTION.

were not used in earlier helicopters because the center of pressure location moved too much when angle of attack was changed. When center of pressure moves, a twisting force is exerted on the rotor blades. Rotor system components had to be designed that would withstand the twisting force. Recent design processes and new materials used to manufacture rotor systems have partially overcome the problems associated with use of nonsymmetrical airfoils.

AIRFOIL SECTIONS

Rotary-wing airfoils operate under diverse conditions, because their speeds are a combination of blade rotation and forward movement of the helicopter. An intelligent discussion of the factors affecting the magnitude of rotor blade lift and drag requires a knowledge of blade section geometry. Blades are designed with specific geometry that adapts them to the varying conditions of flight. Cross-section shapes of most rotor blades are not the same throughout the span. Shapes are varied along the blade radius to take advantage of the particular airspeed range experienced at each point on the blade, and to help balance the load between the root and tip. The blade may be built with a twist, so an airfoil section near the root has a larger pitch angle than a section near the tip.

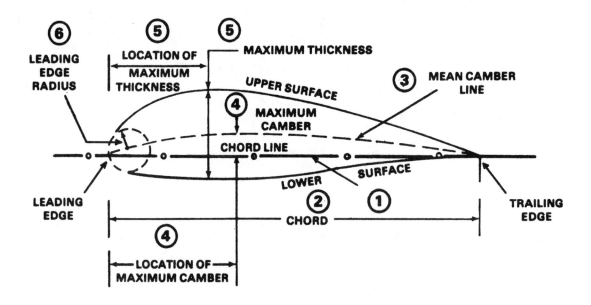

FIGURE 2-10. AIRFOIL TERMINOLOGY.

Figure 2-10 illustrates a typical airfoil section and defines the various items of airfoil terminology.

① The *chord line* is a straight line connecting the leading and trailing edges of the airfoil.

② The *chord* is the length of the chord line from leading edge to trailing edge and is the characteristic longitudinal dimension of the airfoil.

③ The *mean camber line* is a line drawn halfway between the upper and lower surfaces. The chord line connects the ends of the mean camber line.

④ The shape of the mean camber is important in determining the aerodynamic characteristics of an airfoil section. *Maximum camber* (displacement of the mean camber line from the chord line) and the location of maximum camber help to define the shape of the mean camber line. These quantities are expressed as fractions or percentages of the basic chord dimension.

⑤ Thickness and thickness distribution of the profile are important properties of an airfoil section. The *maximum thickness* and its *location* help define the airfoil shape and are expressed as a percentage of the chord.

⑥ The *leading edge radius* of the airfoil is the radius of curvature given the leading edge shape.

ROTARY-WING PLANFORM

Common terms used to describe the helicopter rotor system are shown in figures 2-11 and 2-12. Although there is some variation in systems between different aircraft, the terms shown are generally

2-10

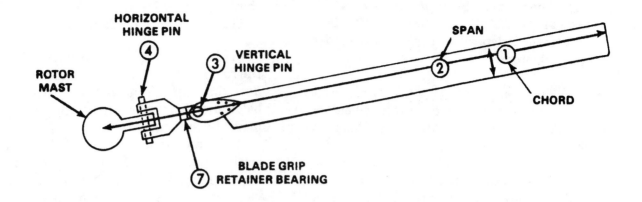

FIGURE 2-11. FULLY ARTICULATED ROTOR SYSTEM.

accepted by most manufacturers. The system shown in figure 2-11 is fully articulated. Semirigid types (fig 2-12) do not have a vertical or horizontal hinge pin. Instead the rotor is allowed to teeter or flap by a trunnion bearing that connects the yoke to the mast.

① The *chord* is the longitudinal dimension of an airfoil section, measured from the leading edge to the trailing edge.

② The *span* is the length of the rotor blade from the point of rotation to the tip of the blade.

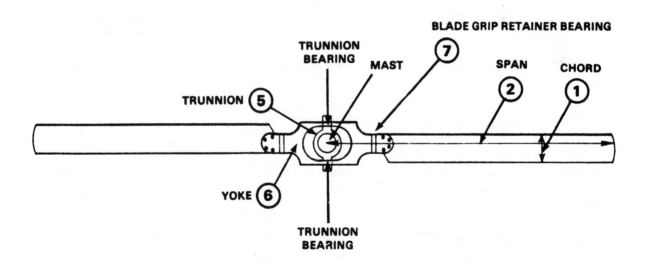

FIGURE 2-12. SEMIRIGID ROTOR SYSTEM.

③ The *vertical hinge pin* (drag hinge) is the axis which permits fore and aft blade movement independent of the other blades in the system.

④ The *horizontal hinge pin* is the axis which permits up and down movement of the blade independent of the other blades in the system.

⑤ The *trunnion* is splined to the mast and has two bearings through which it is secured to the yoke ⑥. The blades are mounted to the yoke and are free to teeter (flap) about the trunnion bearings.

⑥ The *yoke* is the structural member to which the blades are attached and which fastens the rotor blades to the mast through the trunnion and trunnion bearings.

⑦ The *blade grip retainer bearing* is the bearing which permits rotation of the blade

about its spanwise axis, so blade pitch can be changed (blade feathering).

Blade twist is a characteristic built into the rotor blade so angle of incidence is less near the tip than at the root. Blade twist helps distribute the lift evenly along the blade by an increased angle of incidence near the root where blade speed is slower. Outboard portions of the blade that travel faster normally have lower angles of incidence, so less lift is concentrated near the blade tip.

RELATIVE WIND

A knowledge of relative and wind is particularly essential for an understanding of aerodynamics of rotary-wing flight because relative wind may be composed of multiple components. Relative wind is defined as the airflow relative to an airfoil and is illustrated in figure 2-13.

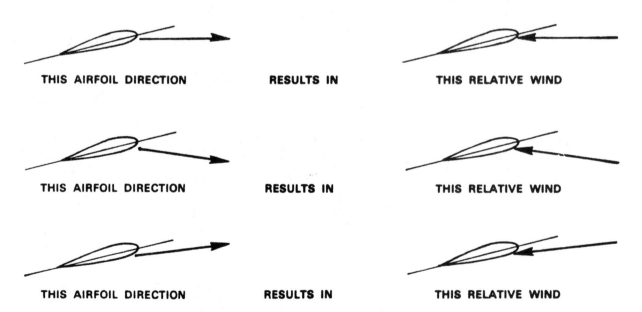

THIS AIRFOIL DIRECTION   RESULTS IN   THIS RELATIVE WIND

THIS AIRFOIL DIRECTION   RESULTS IN   THIS RELATIVE WIND

THIS AIRFOIL DIRECTION   RESULTS IN   THIS RELATIVE WIND

FIGURE 2-13. RELATIVE WIND.

Relative wind is created by movement of an airfoil through the air. As an example, consider a person sitting in an automobile on a no-wind day with a hand extended out the window. There is no airflow about the hand since the automobile is not moving. However, if the automobile is driven at 50 miles per hour, the air will flow under and over the hand at 50 miles per hour. A relative wind has been created by moving the hand through the air. Relative wind flows in the opposite direction that the hand is moving. The velocity of airflow around the hand in motion is the hand's airspeed.

When the helicopter is stationary on a no-wind day, *rotational relative wind* is produced by rotation of the rotor blades. Since the rotor is moving horizontally, the effect is to displace some of the air downward. The blades travel along the same path and pass a given point in rapid succession (a three-bladed system rotating at 320 revolutions per minute (RPM) passes a blade by a given point in the tip-path plane 16 times per second). Figure 2-14 illustrates how still air is changed to a column of descending air by rotor blade action. This flow of air is called an *induced flow* (downwash). It is most predominant at a hover under still wind conditions. Because the rotor system circulates the airflow down through the rotor disk, the rotational relative wind (A, fig 2-15) is modified by the induced flow. Airflow from rotation, modified by induced flow, produces the *resultant relative wind* (D, fig 2-15). In the example shown in D, figure 2-15, angle of attack is reduced by induced flow, causing the airfoil to produce less lift.

When the helicopter has horizontal motion, the resultant relative wind discussed above is further changed by the helicopter airspeed. Airspeed component of relative wind results from the helicopter moving through the air. It is added to or subtracted from the rotational relative wind, depending on whether the blade is advancing or retreating in relation to helicopter movement (B and C, fig 2-15). Induced flow is also modified by introduction of airspeed relative wind. The pattern

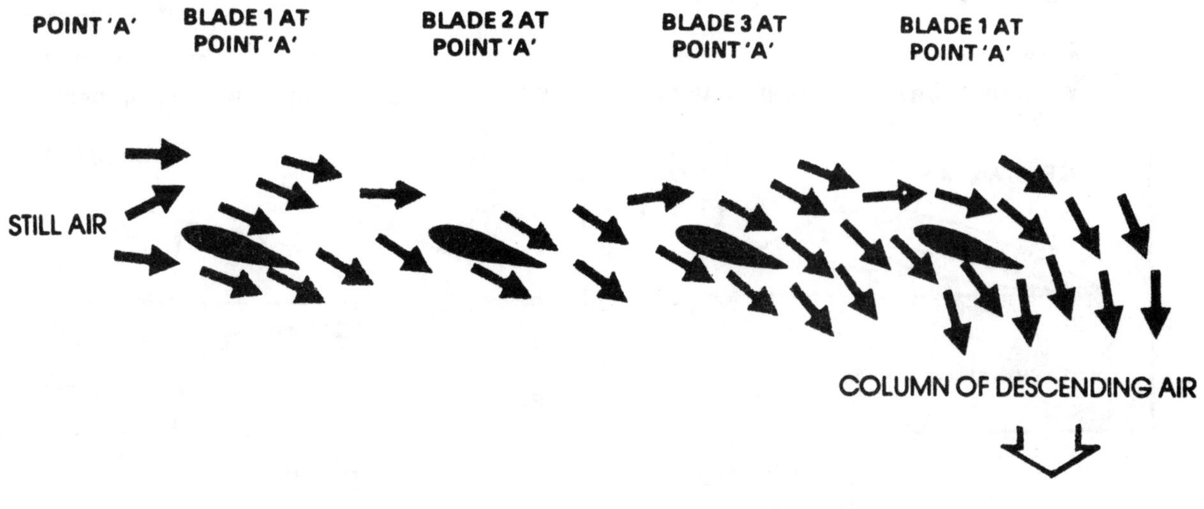

POINT 'A'   BLADE 1 AT POINT 'A'   BLADE 2 AT POINT 'A'   BLADE 3 AT POINT 'A'   BLADE 1 AT POINT 'A'

STILL AIR

COLUMN OF DESCENDING AIR

FIGURE 2-14. INDUCED FLOW (DOWNWASH).

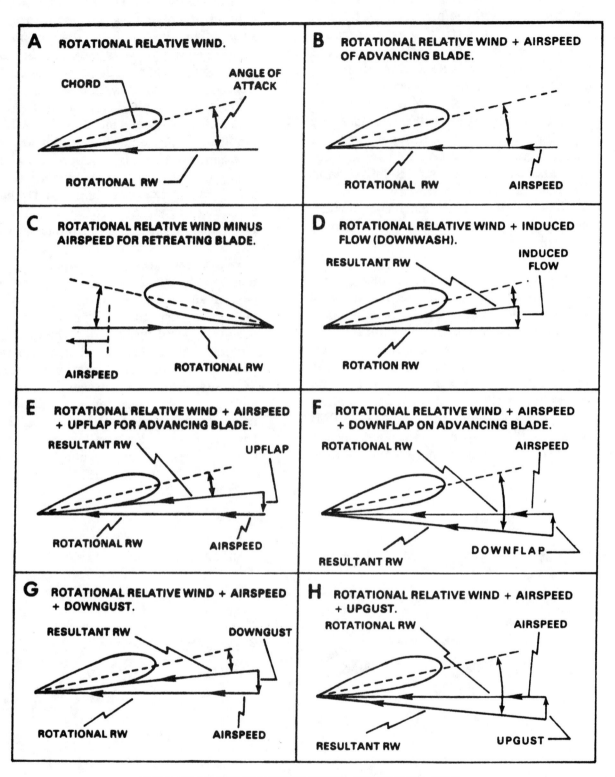

FIGURE 2-15. COMPONENTS OF RELATIVE WIND (RW).

of air circulation through the disk changes when the aircraft has movement. Generally the downward velocity of induced flow is reduced. The helicopter moves continually into an undisturbed airmass, resulting in less time to develop a vertical airflow pattern. As a result, additional lift is produced from a given blade pitch setting. The effects of blade flapping and wind gusts on the relative wind are illustrated in E, F, G, and H (fig 2-15).

ANGLE OF ATTACK

Angle of attack is an *aerodynamic angle* and is illustrated by ④, figure 2-16. It is defined as the angle between the airfoil chord and its direction of motion relative to the air (resultant relative wind). Several factors may cause rotor blade angle of attack to change. Some are controlled by the pilot and some occur automatically due to the rotor system design. Pilots are able to adjust angle of attack by moving the cyclic and collective pitch controls. However, even when these controls are held stationary, the angle of attack constantly changes as the blade moves about the circumference of the rotor disk. Other factors affecting angle of attack, over which the pilot has little control, are blade flapping, blade flexing, and gusty wind or turbulent air conditions. Angle of attack is one of the primary factors that determines amount of lift and drag produced by an airfoil.

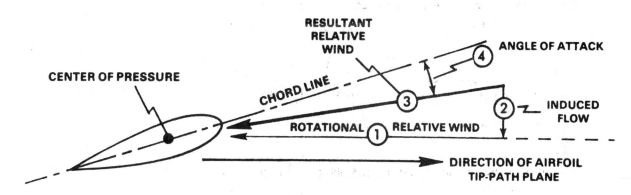

FIGURE 2-16. ANGLE OF ATTACK.

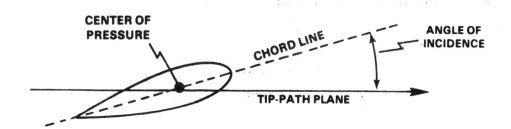

FIGURE 2-17. ANGLE OF INCIDENCE.

Angle of attack should not be confused with angle of incidence (blade pitch angle). Angle of incidence is the angle between the blade chord line and the plane of rotation of the rotor system (fig 2-17). It is a *mechanical angle* rather than an *aerodynamic angle*. In the absence of induced flow and/or aircraft airspeed, angle of attack and angle of incidence are the same. Whenever relative wind is modified by induced flow or aircraft airspeed, then angle of attack is different than angle of incidence.

TOTAL AERODYNAMIC FORCE

A total aerodynamic force is generated when a stream of air flows over and under an airfoil that is moving through the air. The point at which the air separates to flow about the airfoil is called the point of impact (fig 2-18). A high pressure area or stagnation point is formed at the point of impact. Normally the high pressure area is located at the lower portion of the leading edge, depending on angle of attack. The high pressure area contributes to the overall force produced by the blade.

Figure 2-18 also shows airflow lines that illustrate how the air moves about the airfoil section. Notice that the air is deflected downward as it passes under the airfoil and leaves the trailing edge. Remember Newton's third law which states, "every action has an equal and opposite reaction." Since the air is being deflected downward, an equal and opposite force must be acting upward on the airfoil. This force adds to the total aerodynamic force developed by the airfoil. At very low or zero angles of attack, the deflection force or impact pressure may exert a zero positive force or even a downward or negative force.

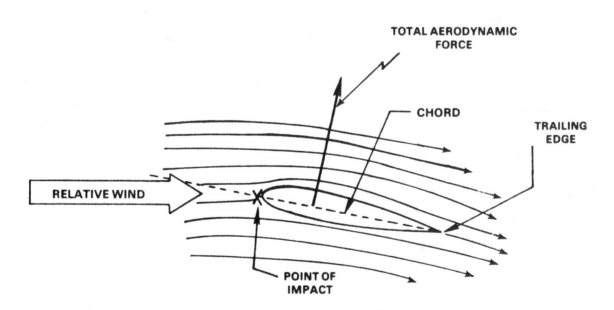

FIGURE 2-18. AIRFLOW AROUND AN AIRFOIL.

Air passing over the top of the airfoil produces aerodynamic force in another way. In figure 2-18, the distance is longer from the point of impact over the top of the airfoil to the trailing edge than the distance from the point of impact to the trailing edge measured under the airfoil. The air traveling over the top must travel further in about the same time as the air traveling under the airfoil. To do this, the air passing over the top must accelerate and travel at a greater velocity. The mass flow equation, already discussed in the section on Bernoulli's Principle, established that pressure and velocity are inversely proportional. Therefore, the increase in velocity causes a decrease in pressure on top of the airfoil and exerts an upward aerodynamic force. Pressure differential between the upper and lower surface of the airfoil is quite small—in the vicinity of 1 percent. Even a small pressure differential produces substantial force when applied to a large area of rotor blade.

The total aerodynamic force, sometimes called the resultant force, may be divided into two components called lift and drag. *Lift* acts on the airfoil in a direction perpendicular to the relative wind and is illustrated by the vector labeled ① (fig 2-19). *Drag* is the resistance or force that opposes the motion of the airfoil through the air. It acts on the airfoil in a direction parallel to the relative wind. Drag is illustrated by the vector labeled ② in figure 2-19.

Many factors contribute to the total lift produced by an airfoil. Increased speed causes increased lift because a larger pressure differential is produced between the upper and lower surfaces. Lift does not increase in direct proportion to speed, but varies as the square of the speed. Thus, a blade traveling at 500 knots has four times the lift of the same blade traveling at only 250 knots. Lift also varies with the area of the blades. A blade area of 100 square feet

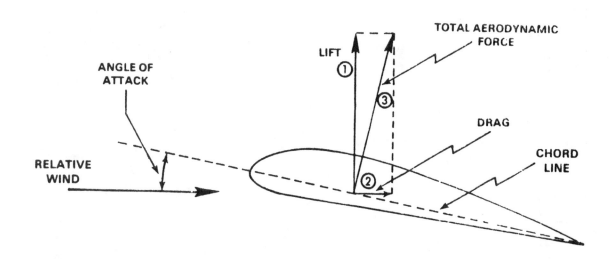

FIGURE 2-19. FORCES ACTING ON AN AIRFOIL.

2-17

will produce twice as much lift as a blade area of only 50 square feet. Angle of attack also has an effect on the lift produced. Lift increases as the angle of attack increases up to the stalling angle of attack. Stall angle varies with different blades and is the point at which airflow no longer follows the camber of the blade smoothly. Camber or shape of the airfoil also has an effect on lift as already discussed in the section on airfoils. Air density is another factor that directly influences lift as covered in the section on properties of the atmosphere.

Two design factors, *airfoil shape* and *airfoil area*, are primary elements that determine how much lift and drag a blade will produce. Any change in these design factors will affect the forces produced. This can best be seen by examination of the following equations:

☐ Lift Equation: $L = C_L\, q\, S$

$$L = C_L\, {\textstyle\frac{1}{2}}\, \rho\, V^2 S$$

Where: L = Lift in pounds

C_L = Coefficient of lift

c = Density of air in slugs/ cubic feet

S = Total blade area in square feet

V = Airspeed in feet per second

q = Dynamic pressure

☐ Drag Equation: $D = C_D\, q\, S$

$$D = C_D\, {\textstyle\frac{1}{2}}\, \rho\, V^2 S$$

Where: D = Drag in pounds

C_D = Coefficient of drag

ρ = Density of air in slugs/ cubic feet

S = Total blade area in square feet

V = Airspeed in feet per second

q = Dynamic pressure

NOTE: C_L and C_D are pure numbers (dimensionless) and are indicative of the effeciency of an airfoil. They are determined from wind tunnel tests and their values vary with different types of airfoils and different angles of attack.

Normally an increase in lift will also produce an increase in drag. Therefore, the airfoil is designed to produce the most lift and the least drag within normal speed ranges. Figure 2-20 shows how lift and drag increase with angle of attack for one type of airfoil. The line labeled L/D shows how the lift/drag ratio varies with different angles of attack.

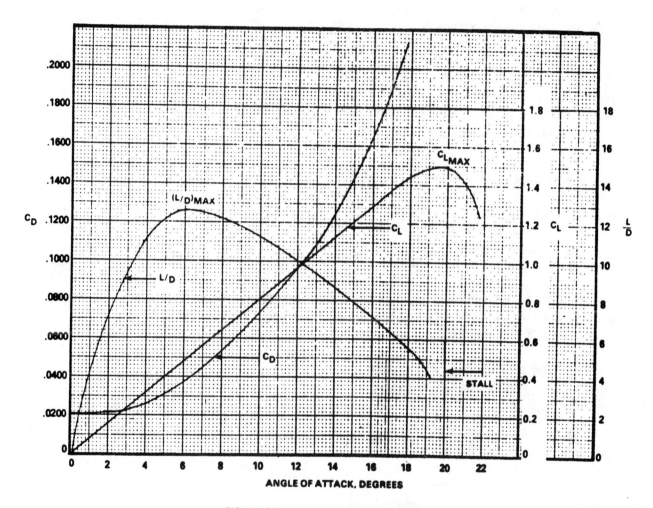

FIGURE 2-20. LIFT-DRAG RELATIONSHIP.

PRESSURE PATTERNS

Distribution of pressure over an airfoil section may be a source of an aerodynamic twisting force as well as lift. A typical example is illustrated by the pressure distribution pattern developed by the cambered (nonsymmetrical) airfoil in figure 2-21. The upper surface has pressures distributed which produce the upper surface lift. The lower surface has pressures distributed which produce the lower surface force. Net lift produced by the airfoil is the difference between lift on the upper surface and the force on the lower surface. Net lift is effectively concentrated at a point on the chord called the *center of pressure*.

When angle of attack is increased (B, fig 2-21), upper surface lift increases relative to the lower surface force. Since the two vectors are not located at the same point along the chord line, a twisting force is exerted about the center of pressure. Center of pressure also moves along the chord line when angle of attack changes, because the two vectors are separated. This characteristic of nonsymmetrical airfoils results in undesirable control forces that must be compensated for if the airfoil is used in rotary-wing applications.

Pressure patterns for symmetrical airfoils are distributed differently than for nonsymmetrical airfoils (fig 2-22). Upper and lower surface vectors are opposite each other instead of being separated along the chord line as in the cambered airfoil in figure 2-21. When the angle of attack is increased to develop positive lift, the vectors remain essentially opposite each other and the twisting force is not exerted. Center of pressure remains relatively constant even when angle of attack is changed. This is a desirable characteristic for a rotor blade, because it changes angle of attack constantly during each revolution.

DRAG

Drag is the force that opposes the motion of an aircraft through the air. *Total drag* produced by an aircraft is the sum of the *profile* drag, *induced* drag, and *parasite* drag described below. Total drag is primarily a function of airspeed. The airspeed that produces the lowest total drag normally determines the aircraft best-rate-of-climb speed, minimum rate-of-descent speed for autorotation, and maximum endurance speed. Figure 2-23 illustrates the interrelationship of these factors.

☐ *Profile drag* is the drag incurred from frictional resistance of the blades passing through the air. It does not change significantly with angle of attack of the airfoil section, but increases moderately as airspeed increases.

☐ *Induced drag* is that drag incurred as a result of production of lift. Higher angles of attack which produce more lift also produce increased induced drag. In rotary-wing aircraft, induced drag decreases with increased aircraft airspeed.

☐ *Parasite drag* is that drag incurred from the nonlifting portions of the aircraft. It includes the form drag and skin friction associated with the fuselage, cockpit, engine cowlings, rotor hub, landing gear, and tail boom. Parasite drag increases with airspeed.

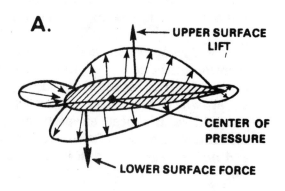

CAMBERED AIRFOIL
AT ZERO LIFT

A.

UPPER SURFACE LIFT

CENTER OF PRESSURE

LOWER SURFACE FORCE

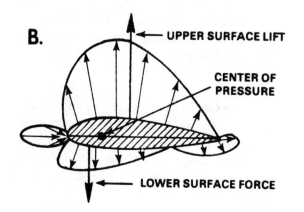

CAMBERED AIRFOIL
AT POSITIVE LIFT

B.

UPPER SURFACE LIFT

CENTER OF PRESSURE

LOWER SURFACE FORCE

FIGURE 2-21. CAMBERED AIRFOIL PRESSURE PATTERNS.

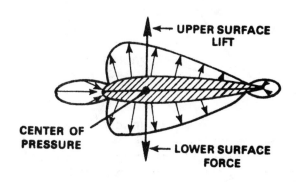

SYMMETRICAL AIRFOIL
AT ZERO LIFT

UPPER SURFACE LIFT

CENTER OF PRESSURE

LOWER SURFACE FORCE

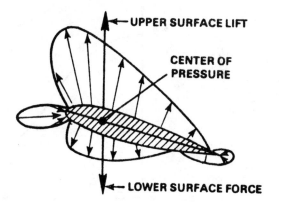

SYMMETRICAL AIRFOIL
AT POSITIVE LIFT

UPPER SURFACE LIFT

CENTER OF PRESSURE

LOWER SURFACE FORCE

FIGURE 2-22. SYMMETRICAL AIRFOIL PRESSURE PATTERNS.

● Curve A shows that parasite drag is very low at slow airspeeds and increases with higher airspeeds. Parasite drag goes up at an increasing rate at airspeeds above the midrange.

● Curve B illustrates how induced drag decreases as aircraft airspeed increases. At a hover, or at lower airspeeds, induced drag is highest. It decreases as airspeed increases and the helicopter moves into undisturbed air.

● Curve C shows the profile drag curve. Profile drag remains relatively constant throughout the speed range with some increase at the higher airspeeds.

● Curve D shows total drag and represents the sum of the other three curves. It identifies the airspeed range, line E, at which total drag is lowest. That airspeed is the best airspeed range for maximum endurance, best rate of climb, and minimum rate of descent in autorotation.

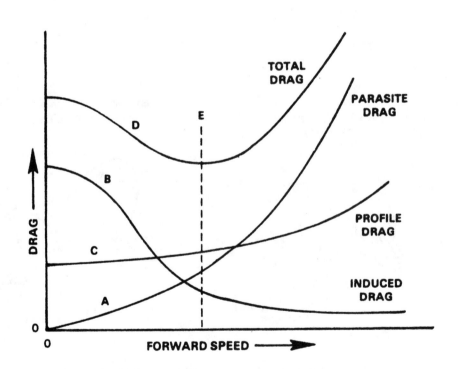

FIGURE 2-23. DRAG/AIRSPEED RELATIONSHIP.

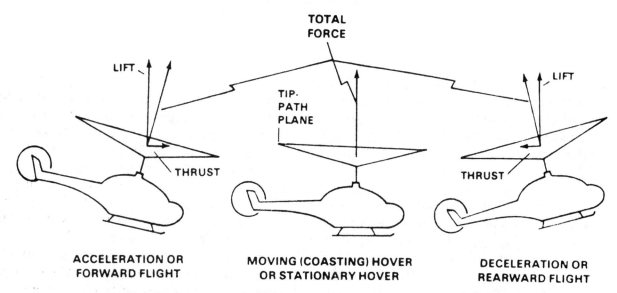

FIGURE 2-24. TOTAL FORCE IS PERPENDICULAR TO TIP-PATH PLANE.

BALANCE OF FORCES

Newton's second law is probably one of the most important principles governing helicopter motion. It states that the rate of change of motion of a body is directly proportional to the applied unbalanced force, and inversely proportional to the body's mass. This means that motion is started, stopped, or changed by causing the forces acting on the body to be unbalanced. Rate of change (acceleration) depends on the magnitude of the unbalanced force and on the mass of the body to which it is applied. Applying this principle

to a helicopter provides the basis for all helicopter flight—vertical, forward, backward, sideward, or hovering. In each case, the *total force* generated by a rotor system is always *perpendicular to the tip-path plane*. For convenience this force is divided into two components—*lift* and *thrust*. The lift component acts to support aircraft weight. The thrust component acts horizontally to accelerate or decelerate the helicopter in the desired direction. Pilots may direct the thrust in the desired direction by tilting the tip-path plane (fig 2-24).

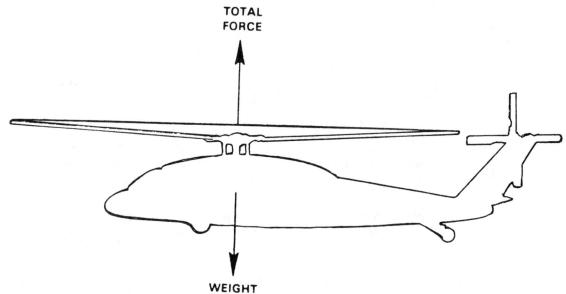

FIGURE 2-25. BALANCED FORCES, HELICOPTER HOVERING, NO WIND.

2-23

At a hover in a no-wind condition, all opposing forces are in balance and the helicopter remains stationary (fig 2-25). The total force is acting opposite to the aircraft weight. To make the helicopter move in some direction, a force must be applied to cause an unbalanced condition. Figure 2-26 shows the unbalanced condition. The pilot has changed the attitude of the rotor disk so there is a lift vector and a thrust vector which results in a total force that is forward of the vertical. No parasite drag is shown because the aircraft has not started to move forward. As the aircraft begins to move (accelerate) in the direction of the applied force (thrust), it begins to develop parasite drag. When parasite drag increases enough and is equal to the thrust,

the body will no longer accelerate because the forces are again in balance (fig 2-27). The aircraft continues to move in the new direction at the new speed until some other unbalance of force is applied to change the motion.

If the pilot wants to return to a hover condition, the aircraft attitude is changed so the thrust vector is smaller than parasite drag, or directed to the rear as shown in figure 2-28. Thrust and parasite drag now act opposite the forward motion so an unbalance of forces exists. The helicopter will decelerate until all motion is stopped. To remain stopped, the pilot must adjust aircraft attitude to balance the forces as shown in figure 2-25.

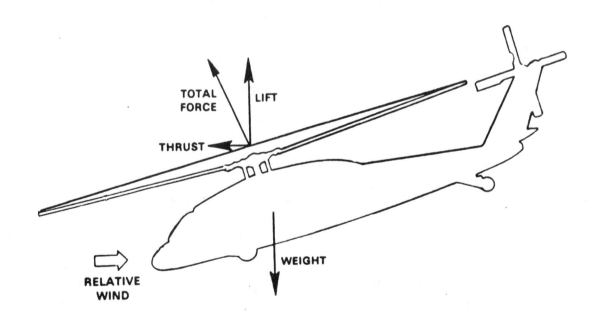

FIGURE 2-26. UNBALANCED FORCES CAUSING ACCELERATION.

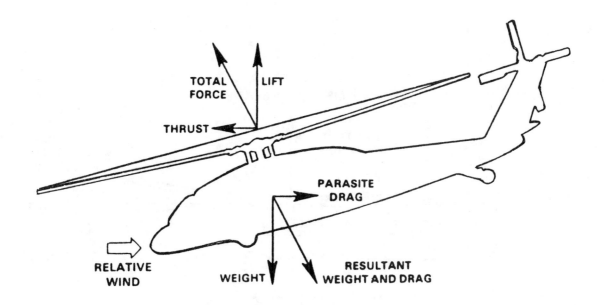

FIGURE 2-27. BALANCED FORCES, AIRCRAFT IN MOTION.

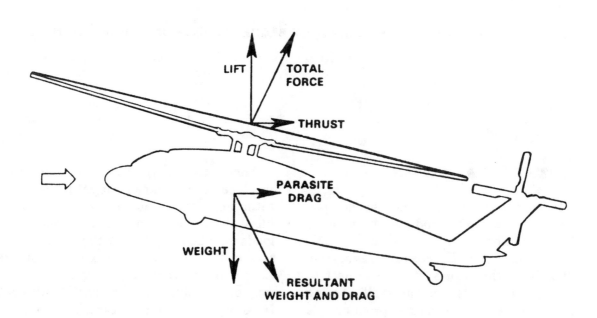

FIGURE 2-28. UNBALANCED FORCES CAUSING DECELERATION.

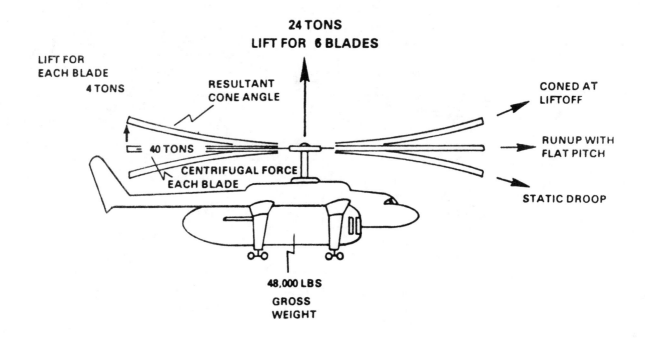

FIGURE 2-29. FLEXIBLE ROTOR BLADES SUPPORTING HEAVY LOAD.

CENTRIFUGAL FORCE

Helicopter rotor systems depend primarily on rotation to produce relative wind which develops the aerodynamic force required for flight. Because of its rotation and weight, the rotor system is subject to forces and moments peculiar to all rotating masses. One of the forces produced is *centrifugal force*. It is defined as the force that tends to make rotating bodies move away from the center of rotation. Another force produced in the rotor system is *centripetal force*. It is the force that counteracts centrifugal force by keeping an object a certain radius from the axis of rotation.

The rotating blades of a helicopter produce very high centrifugal loads on the rotor head and blade attachment assemblies. As a matter of interest, centrifugal loads may be from 6 to 12 tons at the blade root of two to four passenger helicopters. Larger helicopters may develop up to 40 tons of centrifugal load on each blade root. In rotary-wing aircraft, centrifugal force is the dominant force affecting the rotor system. All other forces act to modify this force.

When the rotor blades are at rest, they droop due to their weight and span. In fully articulated systems, they rest against a static or droop stop which prevents the blade from descending so low it will strike the aircraft (fig 2-29). When the rotor system begins to turn, the blade starts to rise from the static position because of centrifugal force. At operating speed, the blades extend straight out even though they are at flat pitch and are not producing lift (fig 2-29).

As the helicopter develops lift during takeoff and flight, the blades rise above the "straight out" position and assume a *coned* position (fig 2-29). Amount of coning depends on RPM, gross weight, and G-forces experienced during flight. If RPM is held constant, coning increases as gross weight and G-force increase. If gross weight and G-forces are constant, decreasing RPM will also cause increased coning. Excessive coning can occur if RPM gets too low, gross weight is too high, or if excessive G-forces are experienced. Excessive coning can cause undersirable stresses on the blade and a decrease of total lift because of a decrease in effective disk area (fig 2-30). Notice that the effective diameter of the rotor disk with increased coning (A, fig 2-30) is less than the diameter of disk B with less coning. A smaller disk diameter has less potential to produce lift.

Centrifugal force and lift effects on the blade can be illustrated best by a vector. Figure 2-31 shows a rotor shaft and vector

resulting from rotation of a blade. Figure 2-32 shows a vertical force vector acting at the blade tip. This vertical force is lift produced when the blades assume a positive angle of attack. The blade is no longer being acted upon solely by centrifugal force. It is also producing lift which is manifested at the blade tip by the lift vector. Since one end of the blade is attached to the rotor shaft, it is not free to move. The other end can move and will assume a position that is a resultant of the forces (vectors) acting on it (fig 2-33). The blade position is coned and is a resultant of two forces, lift and centrifugal force.

FIGURE 2-31. CENTRIFUGAL FORCE.

FIGURE 2-32. LIFT AND CENTRIFUGAL FORCE.

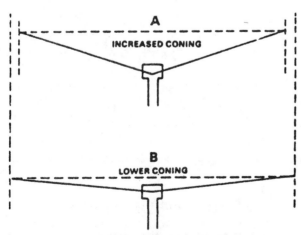

FIGURE 2-30. LOSS OF DISK AREA DUE TO CONING.

FIGURE 2-33. RESULTANT OF LIFT AND CENTRIFUGAL FORCES.

ROTATIONAL VELOCITIES

During hovering, airflow over the rotor blades is produced by rotation of the rotor system. Figure 2-34 shows a typical helicopter rotor system. An arbitrary rotor diameter of 40 feet and rotor speed of 320 revolutions per minute is used to illustrate typical rotational velocities. Blade tip velocity for this rotor is 670 feet per second which converts to 397 knots.

Blade speed near the main rotor shaft is much less because the distance traveled at the smaller radius is relatively small. At point A, figure 2-34, half way from the rotor shaft to the blade tip, the blade speed is only 198.5 knots which is one-half the tip speed. Speed at any point on the blades varies with the radius or distance from the center of the main rotor shaft. An extreme airspeed differential between the blade tip and root is the result. The lift differential between the blade root and tip is even larger because lift varies as the square of the speed. Therefore, when speed is doubled, lift is increased four times. This means that the lift at point A, figure 2-34, would be only one-fourth as much as lift at the blade tip (assuming the airfoil shape and angle of attack are the same at both points).

Because of the potential lift differential along the blade resulting primarily from speed variation, blades are designed with a twist. Blade twist provides a higher pitch angle at the root where speed is low and lower pitch angles nearer the tip where speed is higher. This design helps distribute the lift more evenly along the blade. It increases both the induced air velocity and the blade loading near the inboard section of the blade. Figure 2-35 compares the lift of a twisted and untwisted blade. Note that the twisted blade generates more lift near the root and less lift at the tip than the untwisted blade.

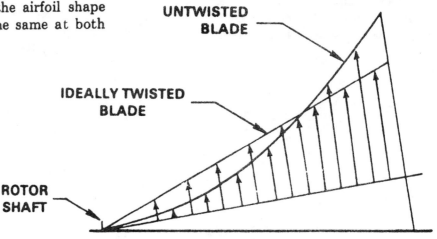

FIGURE 2-35. DISTRIBUTION OF LIFT ON TWISTED AND UNTWISTED BLADE.

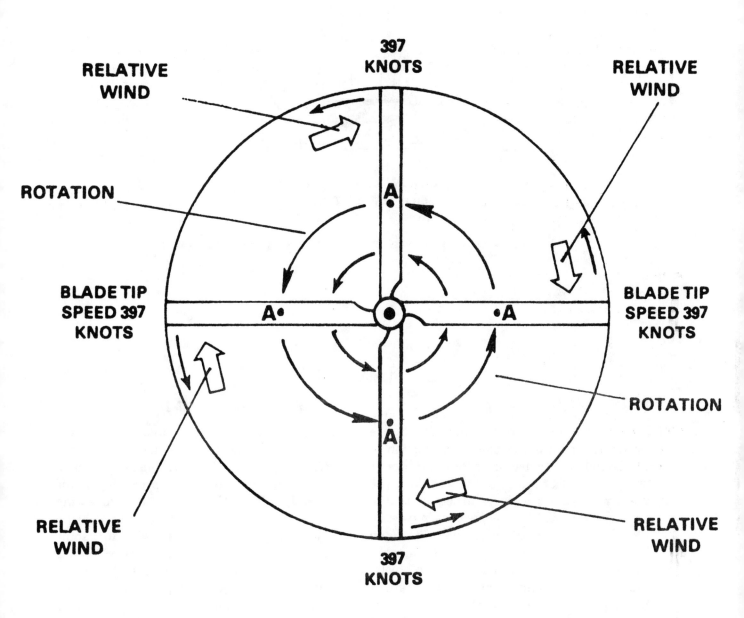

FIGURE 2-34. BLADE SPEED AT HOVER.

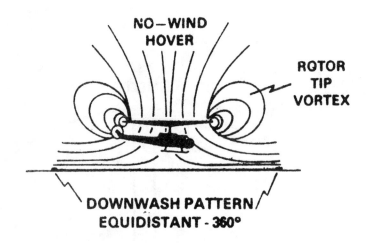

NO—WIND
HOVER

ROTOR
TIP
VORTEX

DOWNWASH PATTERN
EQUIDISTANT - 360°

FIGURE 2-36. ROTOR TIP VORTEX AT A HOVER.

HOVERING

Hovering is the term applied when a helicopter maintains a constant position at a selected point, usually a few feet above the ground. For a helicopter to hover, the main rotor must supply lift equal to the total weight of the helicopter. With the blades rotating at high velocity, an increase of blade pitch (angle of attack) would induce the necessary lift for a hover. The forces of lift and weight reach a state of balance during the stationary hover.

Hovering is actually an element of vertical flight. Assuming a no-wind condition, the tip-path plane of the blades will remain horizontal. If the angle of attack of the blades is increased while their velocity remains constant, additional vertical thrust is obtained. Thus, by upsetting the vertical balance of forces, the helicopter will climb vertically. By the same principle, the reverse is true; decreased pitch will result in the helicopter descending.

AIRFLOW DURING HOVERING

At a hover, the rotor tip vortex (air swirl at the tip of the rotor blades) reduces the effectiveness of the outer blade portions. Also, the vortexes of the preceding blade severely affect the lift of the following blades. If the vortex made by one passing blade remains a vicious swirl for some number of seconds, then two blades operating at 350 RPM create 700 long-lasting vortex patterns per minute. This continuous creation of new vortexes and ingestion of existing vortexes is the primary cause of high power requirements for hovering (fig 2-36).

During hover, the rotor blades move large volumes of air in a downward direction. This pumping process uses lots of horsepower and accelerates the air to relatively high velocities. Air velocity under the helicopter may reach 60 to 100 knots, depending on the size and gross weight. The flow pattern and an airfoil

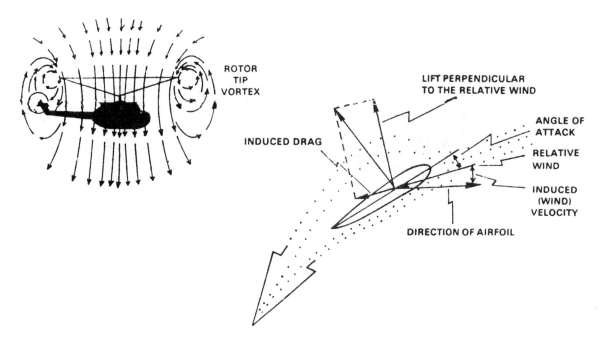

FIGURE 2-37. OUT-OF-GROUND-EFFECT HOVER.

section for a helicopter hovering out-of-ground-effect are shown in figure 2-37. Note how the downwash (induced flow) of air has introduced another element into the relative wind which alters the angle of attack of the airfoil. When there is no induced flow, the relative wind is opposite and parallel to the flightpath of the airfoil. In this case, the downward airflow (induced wind velocity) alters the relative wind and changes the angle of attack so less aerodynamic force is produced. This condition requires the pilot to increase collective pitch to produce enough aerodynamic force to sustain a hover.

GROUND EFFECT

The high power requirement needed to hover out-of-ground-effect (fig 2-37) is reduced when operating in ground effect (fig 2-38). Ground effect is a condition of improved performance encountered when operating near the ground. It is due to interference of the surface with the airflow pattern of the rotor system; and it is more pronounced the nearer the ground is approached. Increased blade efficiency while operating in ground effect is due to two separate and distinct phenomena as follows:

□ First, and most important, is the reduction of the velocity of the induced airflow. Since the ground interrupts the airflow under the helicopter, the entire flow is altered. This reduces downward velocity of the induced flow. The result is less induced drag and a more vertical lift vector. The lift needed to sustain a hover can be produced with a reduced angle of attack and less power because of the more vertical lift vector (fig 2-38).

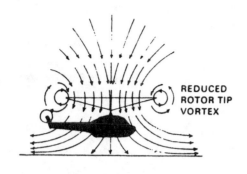

REDUCED ROTOR TIP VORTEX

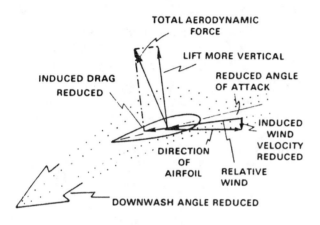

TOTAL AERODYNAMIC FORCE

LIFT MORE VERTICAL

INDUCED DRAG REDUCED

REDUCED ANGLE OF ATTACK

INDUCED WIND VELOCITY REDUCED

DIRECTION OF AIRFOIL

RELATIVE WIND

DOWNWASH ANGLE REDUCED

FIGURE 2-38. IN-GROUND-EFFECT HOVER.

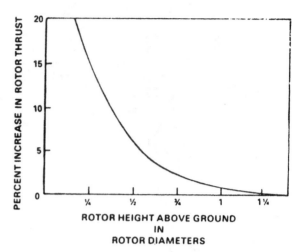

FIGURE 2-39. INCREASED LIFT CAPABILITY IN-GROUND-EFFECT.

☐ The second phenomena is a reduction of the rotor *tip vortex* (fig 2-38). When operating in-ground-effect, the downward and outward airflow pattern tends to restrict vortex generation. This makes the outboard portion of the rotor blade more efficient and reduces overall system turbulence caused by ingestion and recirculation of the vortex swirls.

Rotor efficiency is increased by ground effect up to a height of about one rotor diameter for most helicopters. Figure 2-39 illustrates the percent increase in rotor thrust experienced at various rotor heights. At a rotor height of one-half rotor diameter, the thrust is increased about 7 percent.

At rotor heights above one rotor diameter, the thrust increase is small and decreases to zero at a height of about 1 ¼ rotor diameter.

Maximum ground effect is accomplished when hovering over smooth paved surfaces. While hovering over tall grass, rough terrain, revetments, or water, ground effect may be seriously reduced. This phenomena is due to the partial breakdown and cancellation of ground effect and the return of large vortex patterns with increased downwash angles.

Two identical airfoils with equal blade pitch angles are compared in figure 2-40. The top airfoil is out-of-ground-effect while the bottom airfoil is in-ground-effect. The airfoil that is in-ground-effect is more efficient because it operates at a larger angle of attack and produces a more vertical lift vector. Its increased efficiency results from a smaller downward induced

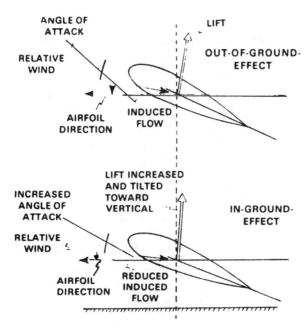

FIGURE 2-40. EFFECT OF GROUND PROXIMITY AT A CONSTANT PITCH ANGLE.

wind velocity which increases angle of attack. The airfoil operating out-of-ground-effect is less efficient because of increased induced wind velocity which reduces angle of attack.

If a helicopter hovering out-of-ground-effect descends into a ground-effect hover, blade efficiency increases because of the more favorable induced flow. As efficiency of the rotor system increases, the pilot reduces blade pitch angle to remain in the ground-effect hover. Less power is required to maintain hover in-ground-effect than for the out-of-ground-effect hover.

TORQUE

In accordance with Newton's law of action and reaction, the helicopter fuselage tends to rotate in the direction opposite to the rotor blades. This effect is called torque ②, figure 2-41. Torque must be counter-

acted and/or controlled before flight is possible. In tandem rotor and coaxial helicopter designs, the rotors turn in opposite directions to neutralize or eliminate torque effect. In tip-jet helicopters, power originates at the blade tip and equal and opposite reaction is against the air; there is no torque between the rotor and the fuselage. However, the torque problem is especially important in single main rotor helicopters with a fuselage-mounted power source. The torque effect on the fuselage (②, fig 2-41) is a direct result of the work/ resistance of the main rotor. Therefore torque is at the geometric center of the main rotor. Torque results from the rotor being driven by the engine power output. Any change in engine power output brings about a corresponding change in torque effect. Furthermore, power varies with the flight maneuver and results in a variable torque effect that must be continually corrected.

ANTITORQUE ROTOR

Compensation for torque in the single main rotor helicopter is accomplished by means of a variable-pitch, antitorque rotor (tail rotor), located on the end of a tail boom extension at the rear of the fuselage. Driven by the main rotor at a constant ratio, the tail rotor produces thrust in a horizontal plane opposite to torque reaction developed by the main rotor (③, fig 2-41). Since torque effect varies during flight when power changes are made, it is necessary to vary the thrust of the tail rotor. Antitorque pedals enable the aviator to compensate for torque variance. A significant part of the engine power is required to drive the tail rotor, especially during operations where maximum power is used. From 5 to 15 percent of the available engine power may be needed to

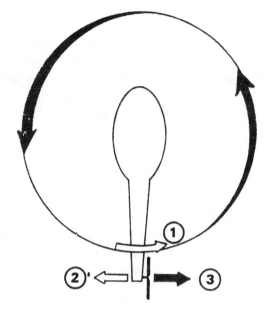

1. Rotation direction of engine-driven main rotor.
2. Torque effect rotates fuselage in direction opposite to main rotor.
3. Tail rotor counteracts torque effect and provides positive fuselage heading control.

FIGURE 2-41. COMPENSATING TORQUE REACTION.

drive the tail rotor depending on helicopter size and design. Normally, larger helicopters use a higher percent of engine power to counteract torque than do smaller aircraft. A helicopter with 9,500 horsepower might require 1,200 horsepower to drive the tail rotor, while a 200 horsepower aircraft might require only 10 horsepower for torque correction.

HEADING CONTROL

In addition to counteracting torque, the tail rotor and its control linkage also permit control of the helicopter heading during taxiing, hovering, and sideslip operations on takeoffs and approaches. Application of

more control than is necessary to counteract torque will cause the nose of the helicopter to swing in the direction of pedal movement (left pedal to the left). Conversely, less pedal than required to counteract torque would permit the helicopter to turn in the direction of torque (i.e., nose would swing to the right). To maintain a constant heading at a hover or during takeoff or approach, an aviator must use antitorque pedals to apply just enough pitch on the tail rotor to neutralize torque and hold a slip if necessary. Heading control in forward trimmed flight is normally accomplished with cyclic control, using a coordinated bank and turn to the desired heading. Application of antitorque pedals will be required when power changes are made.

NOTE: In an autorotation, some degree of right pedal is required to maintain correct pedal trim. When torque is not present, as in an autorotation, mast thrust bearing friction tends to turn the fuselage in the same direction as (or with) the main rotor. To counteract this friction, the tail rotor thrust is at times reversed by the pilot and applied in a direction opposite to that required for torque correction in powered flight.

TRANSLATING TENDENCY

During hovering flight, the single rotor helicopter has a tendency to drift laterally to the right. The tendency results from right lateral tail rotor thrust that is exerted to compensate for main rotor torque (fig 2-42). The pilot may prevent right lateral drift of the helicopter by tilting the main rotor disk to the left. This lateral tilt results in a main rotor force to the left that compensates for the tail rotor thrust to the right.

Helicopter design usually includes one or more features which help the pilot compensate for translating tendency.

☐ Flight control rigging may be designed so the rotor disk is tilted slightly left when the cyclic control is centered.

☐ The main transmission may be mounted so that the mast is tilted slightly to the left when the helicopter fuselage is laterally level.

☐ The collective pitch control system may be designed so that the rotor disk tilts slightly left, as collective pitch is increased to hover aircraft.

FUSELAGE HOVERING ATTITUDE

The design of most fully articulated rotor systems includes an offset between the main rotor mast and the blade attachment point. Centrifugal force acting on the offset tends to hold the mast perpendicular to the tip-path plane (A, fig 2-43). As a result, when the rotor disk is tilted left to counteract translating tendency, the fuselage will follow the main rotor mast and hang slightly low on the left side (B, fig 2-43).

A fuselage suspended under a semirigid rotor system will remain level laterally unless the load is unbalanced or the tail rotor gearbox is lower than the main rotor (B, fig 2-45). The fuselage remains level because there is no offset between the rotor mast and the point where the rotor system is attached to the mast (trunnion bearings).

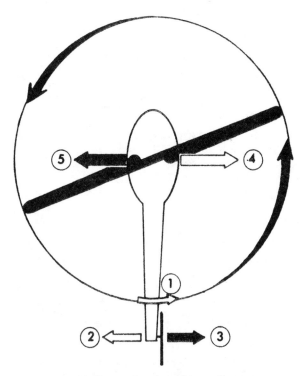

1 Rotation direction of engine-driven main rotor.
2 Torque effect rotates fuselage in direction opposite to main rotor.
3 Tail rotor counteracts torque effect and provides positive fuselage heading control.
4 Tail rotor pulls or pushes entire helicopter into right drift (translating tendency).
5 As necessary to prevent right drift, pilot applies left rotor tilt to counteract translating tendency.

FIGURE 2-42. COMPENSATING FOR
TRANSLATING TENDENCY.

Because the trunnion bearings are centered on the mast, the mast has no tendency to follow the tilt of the rotor disk during hovering (fig 2-44). The mast does not tend to remain perpendicular to the tip-path plane as is true with the fully articulated rotor system. Instead, the mast tends to hang vertically under the trunnion bearings even when the rotor disk is tilted left to compensate for translating tendency (A, fig 2-45). Because the mast remains vertical, the fuselage hangs level laterally unless it is affected by other forces.

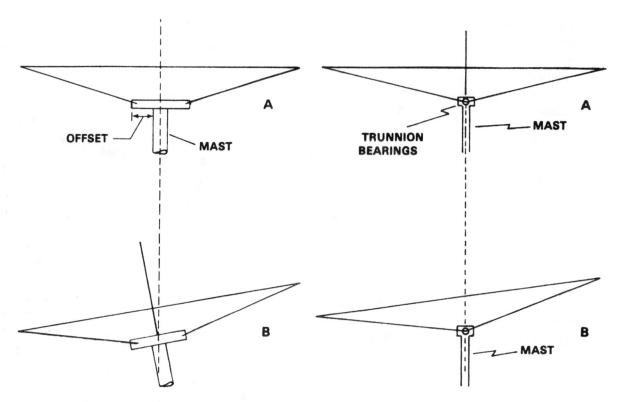

FIGURE 2-43. FULLY ARTICULATED ROTOR
SYSTEM.

FIGURE 2-44. SIMIRIGID ROTOR SYSTEM.

The main rotor mast in semirigid and fully articulated rotor systems may be designed with a forward tilt relative to the fuselage. Forward tilt provides for a level longitudinal fuselage attitude during forward flight (resulting in reduced parasite drag), but results in a tail low fuselage attitude during hovering. When the fuselage is tail low, the tail rotor gearbox will be lower than the main rotor. During hover, this causes a slightly unbalanced couple between the tail rotor and the main rotor which makes the fuselage tilt laterally to the left (B, fig 2-45).

AIRFLOW IN FORWARD FLIGHT

The efficiency of the hovering rotor system is improved with each knot of incoming wind gained by horizontal movement or surface wind. As the incoming wind enters the rotor system, turbulence and vortexes are left behind and the flow of air becomes more horizontal. All of these changes improve the efficiency of the rotor system and improve aircraft performance.

Improved rotor efficiency resulting from directional flight is called *translational lift*. An airflow pattern for a forward speed of 1 to 5 knots is shown in figure 2-46. Note how the downwind vortex is beginning to dissipate and induced flow down through the rear of the rotor disk is more horizontal than at a hover (fig 2-38).

Figure 2-47 shows the airflow pattern at a speed of 10 to 15 knots. Airflow is much more horizontal than at a hover. The leading edge of the downwash pattern is being overrun and is well back under the helicopter nose. At about 16 to 24 knots (depending upon the size, blade area, and RPM of the rotor system) the rotor completely outruns the recirculation of old vortexes and begins to work in relatively clean air. The rotor no longer pumps the air in a circular pattern, but continually flies into undisturbed air. The air passing through the rotor system is nearly horizontal, depending on helicopter forward speed.

As the helicopter speed increases, translational lift becomes more effective and causes the nose to rise, or pitch up (sometimes called blowback). This tendency is caused by the combined effects of dissymmetry of lift and transverse flow which are explained in detail in later paragraphs. Pilots must correct for this

tendency in order to maintain a constant rotor disk attitude that will move the helicopter through the speed range where blowback occurs. If the nose is permitted to pitch up while passing through this speed range, the aircraft may also tend to roll slightly to the right.

When the single main rotor helicopter transitions from hover to forward flight, the tail rotor becomes more aerodynamically efficient. Efficiency increases because the tail rotor works in progressively less turbulent air as speed increases. As tail rotor efficiency improves, more thrust is produced. This causes the aircraft nose to yaw left if the main rotor turns counterclockwise. During a takeoff where power is constant, the pilot must apply right pedal as speed increases to correct for the left yaw tendency.

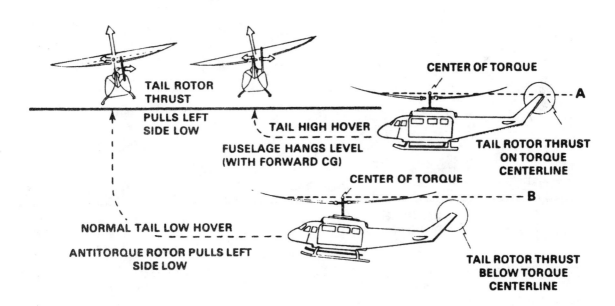

FIGURE 2-45. EFFECT OF TAIL LOW ATTITUDE ON LATERAL HOVER ATTITUDE.

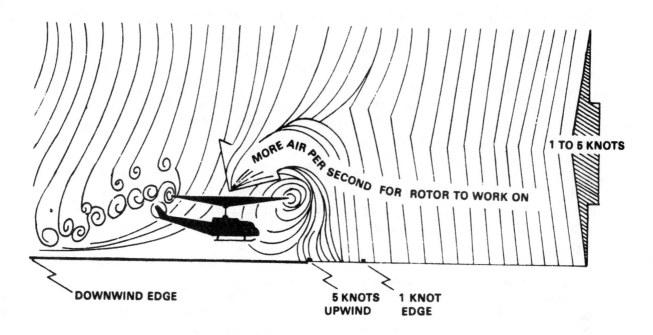

FIGURE 2-46. TRANSLATIONAL LIFT AT 1 to 5 KNOTS.

**AIRFLOW PATTERN JUST PRIOR TO
EFFECTIVE TRANSLATIONAL LIFT**

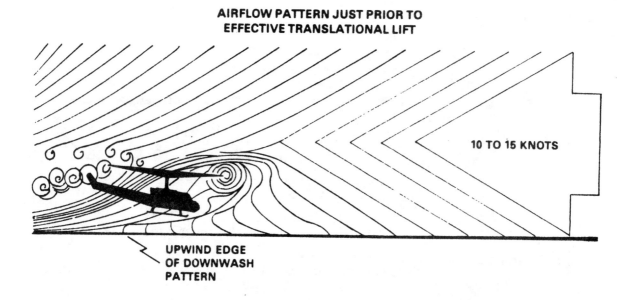

FIGURE 2-47. TRANSLATIONAL LIFT AT 10 TO 15 KNOTS.

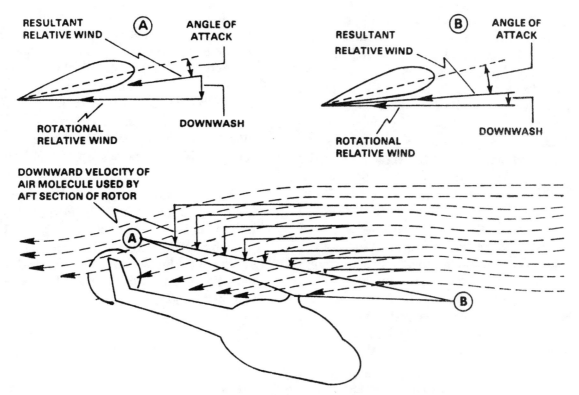

FIGURE 2-48. TRANSVERSE FLOW EFFECT.

TRANSVERSE FLOW EFFECT

In forward flight, air passing through the rear portion of the rotor disk has a greater downwash angle than air passing through the forward portion (fig 2-48). The downward flow at the rear of the rotor disk causes a reduced angle of attack, resulting in less lift. Increased angle of attack, and more lift is produced at the front portion of the disk because airflow is more horizontal. These differences between the fore and aft parts of the rotor disk are called transverse flow effect. They cause unequal drag in the fore and aft parts of the disk resulting in vibrations that are easily recognizable by the pilot. The vibrations are more noticeable for most helicopters between 10 and 20 knots.

DISSYMMETRY OF LIFT

Dissymmetry of lift is the difference in lift that exists between the advancing half of the rotor disk and the retreating half. It is caused by the fact that in directional flight the aircraft relative wind is added to the rotational relative wind on the advancing blade and subtracted on the retreating blade (fig 2-49). The blade passing the tail and advancing around the right side of the helicopter has an increasing airspeed which reaches maximum at the 3 o'clock position. As the blade continues, the airspeed reduces to essentially rotational airspeed over the nose of the helicopter. Leaving the nose, the blade airspeed progressively decreases and reaches minimum airspeed at the 9 o'clock position. The blade airspeed then increases progressively and again reaches rotational airspeed as it passes over the tail.

Note the shaded circle in figure 2-49 labeled "REVERSE FLOW AREA." Blade airspeed at the outboard edge of the shaded circle is 0 knots. Within the reverse flow area, the air actually moves over the blade backwards from trailing edge to leading edge. From the reverse flow area out to the blade tip, the blade airspeed progressively increases up to 294 knots.

At an aircraft airspeed of 100 knots (fig 2-49), a 200-knot blade airspeed differential exists between the advancing and retreating blades. Since lift increases as the square of the airspeed, a potential lift variation exists between the advancing and retreating sides of the rotor disk. This lift

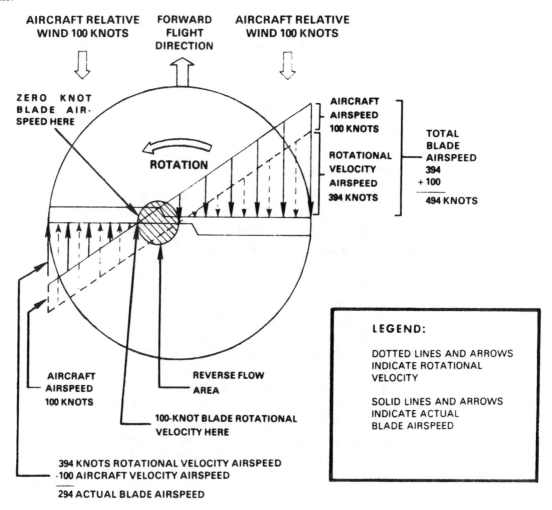

FIGURE 2-49. DISSYMMETRY OF LIFT.

differential must be compensated for, or the helicopter would not be controllable.

To compare the lift of the advancing half of the disk area to the lift of the retreating half, the lift equation discussed earlier can be used. In forward flight, two factors in the lift formula, density ratio (ρ) and blade area (S), are the same for both the advancing and retreating blades. The airfoil shape (one part of C_L) is fixed for a given blade. The only remaining variables are changes in blade angle of attack (another part of C_L) and blade airspeed. These two variables must compensate for each other during forward flight to overcome dissymmetry of lift.

Two factors, *rotor RPM* and *aircraft airspeed*, control blade airspeed during flight. Both factors are variable to some degree, but must remain within certain operating limits specified for the aircraft. Angle of attack remains as the one variable that may be used by the pilot to compensate for dissymmetry of lift. The pitch angle of the rotor blades can be varied throughout their range, from flat pitch to the stalling pitch angle, to change angle of attack and to compensate for lift differential.

Figure 2-50 illustrates the relationship between blade pitch angle and blade airspeed during forward flight. Note that blade pitch angle is lower on the advancing side of the disk to compensate for increased blade airspeed on that side. Blade pitch

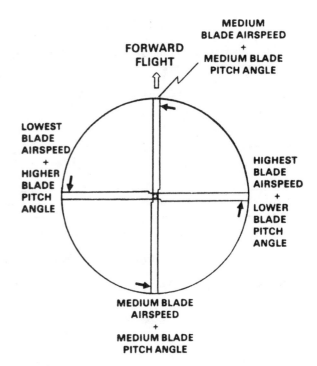

FIGURE 2-50. BLADE PITCH ANGLE VARIATION TO COMPENSATE FOR DISSYMMETRY OF LIFT.

angle is increased on the retreating blade side to compensate for decreased blade airspeed on that side. These changes in blade pitch are introduced through the blade feathering mechanism and are called cyclic feathering. Pitch changes are made to individual blades independent of the others in the system and are controlled by the pilot's cyclic pitch stick.

The tail rotor experiences dissymmetry of lift during forward flight, because it has advancing and retreating blades. Dissymmetry is corrected for by a flapping hinge action. Two basic types of flapping hinges, the *delta* hinge and the *offset* hinge, are used on most contemporary helicopters.

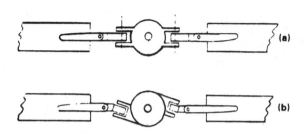

(a) Plain flapping hinge. (b) Delta-three hinge combines flapping and cyclic feathering.

FIGURE 2-51. FLAPPING HINGES.

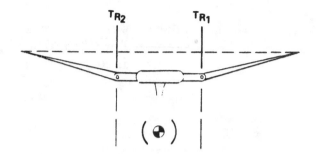

Flapping hinge offset from center produces moments without disk tilt.

FIGURE 2-52. OFFSET FLAPPING HINGE.

The delta hinge is not oriented parallel to the blade chord (fig 2-51). It is designed so flapping automatically introduces cyclic feathering which corrects for dissymmetry of lift. The offset hinge is located outboard from the hub (fig 2-52). The offset hinge uses centrifugal force to produce substantial forces that act on the hub. One important advantage of offset hinges is the presence of control regardless of lift condition, since centrifugal force is independent of lift.

BLADE FLAPPING

Blade flapping is the up and down movement of a rotor blade, and is the primary way of compensating for lift dissymmetry. Flapping action varies, depending on the type rotor system. In the fully articulated rotor system, blades flap individually about a horizontal hinge pin. Each blade is free to move up and down independently from all the other blades.

Semirigid rotor systems flap somewhat differently than fully articulated systems. A blade in a semirigid system is not free to flap independently of the other blade. Instead, if one blade flaps up, the other must flap down, since they move together on a common teetering hinge. Some independent flapping can take place through blade flexing.

Rigid rotor systems have no hinge to permit flapping to take place. They depend entirely on structural bending or flexing to perform the flapping action.

Flapping action corrects for dissymmetry of lift on the advancing side by changing the angle of attack as illustrated in B, figure 2-53. Blade angle of attack over the tail is shown in A, figure 2-53. As the blade moves forward from the tail on the advancing side, blade airspeed begins to increase and produces more lift. The blade responds by climbing (flapping up). Flapping up introduces a vertical vector into the

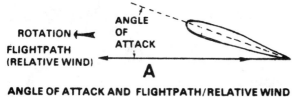

ANGLE OF ATTACK AND FLIGHTPATH/RELATIVE WIND
OVER THE TAIL

A

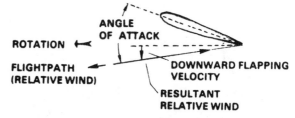

ANGLE OF ATTACK AND FLIGHT-
PATH/RELATIVE WIND OVER NOSE

A

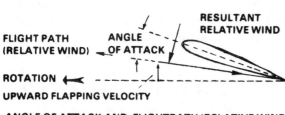

ANGLE OF ATTACK AND FLIGHTPATH/RELATIVE WIND
OVER RIGHT (ADVANCING) SIDE

B

FIGURE 2-53. ANGLE OF ATTACK CHANGES
CAUSED BY FLAPPING.

ANGLE OF ATTACK AND FLIGHTPATH/RELATIVE
WIND OVER LEFT (RETREATING) SIDE

B

FIGURE 2-54. ANGLE OF ATTACK CHANGES
CAUSED BY FLAPPING.

relative wind which effectively decreases the angle of attack (B, fig 2-53). The upward flapping velocity is just enough to reduce angle of attack, so lift is kept essentially constant.

Flapping action on the retreating side of the rotor disk works similarly, except flapping is down instead of up. Angle of attack as the blade passes over the aircraft nose is shown in A, figure 2-54. As the blade moves rearward from the nose on the retreating side, blade airspeed begins to decrease and produces less lift. The blade responds by descending (flapping down). Flapping down introduces a downward velocity into the relative wind which effectively increases the angle of attack,

causing more lift to be produced (B, fig 2-54). Downflapping velocity is just enough to increase the angle of attack, so lift is kept constant.

GYROSCOPIC PRECESSION

Gyroscopic precession is a phenomenon occurring in rotating bodies in which an applied force is manifested 90° ahead in the direction of rotation from where the force was applied. Although precession is not a dominant force in rotary-wing aerodynamics, it must be reckoned with because turning rotor systems exhibit some of the

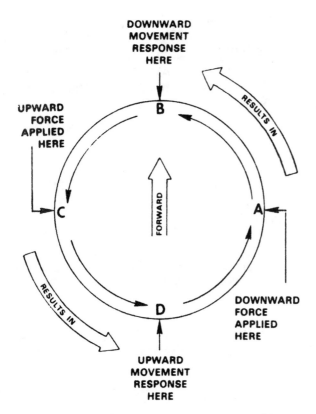

DOWNWARD MOVEMENT RESPONSE HERE

UPWARD FORCE APPLIED HERE

FORWARD

RESULTS IN

RESULTS IN

DOWNWARD FORCE APPLIED HERE

UPWARD MOVEMENT RESPONSE HERE

FIGURE 2-55. GYROSCOPIC PRECESSION.

characteristics of a gyro. Figure 2-55 shows how precession affects the rotor disk when force is applied at a given point. A downward force applied to the disk at point A results in a downward change in disk attitude at point B. An upward force applied at point C results in an upward change in disk attitude at point D.

Forces applied to a spinning rotor disk by control input or by wind gusts will react as follows:

Force Causing
Aircraft Movement   *Aircraft Reaction*
nose up ——————— roll right
nose down——————— roll left
roll right——————— nose up
roll left ——————— nose down

This behavior explains some of the fundamental effects occurring during various helicopter maneuvers. For example, the helicopter behaves differently when rolling into a right turn than when rolling into a left turn. During roll into a left turn, the pilot will have to correct for a nose down tendency in order to maintain altitude. This correction is required because precession causes a nose down tendency and because the tilted disk produces less vertical lift to counteract gravity. Conversely, during a roll into a right turn, precession will cause a nose up tendency while the tilted disk will produce less vertical lift. Pilot input required to maintain altitude is significantly different during a right turn than during a left turn, because gyroscopic precession acts in opposite directions for each.

ROTOR HEAD CONTROL SYSTEMS

☐ *Cyclic and Collective Pitch.* Pilot inputs to the cyclic and collective pitch

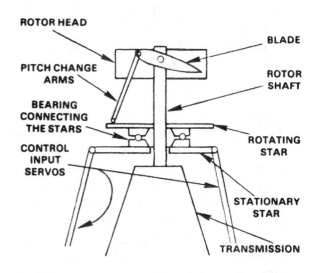

ROTOR HEAD

BLADE

PITCH CHANGE ARMS

ROTOR SHAFT

BEARING CONNECTING THE STARS

CONTROL INPUT SERVOS

ROTATING STAR

STATIONARY STAR

TRANSMISSION

FIGURE 2-56. ROTOR HEAD CONTROL SYSTEM.

controls are transmitted to the rotor blades through a complex system of levers, mixing units, input servos, stationary and rotating stars (swashplates), and pitch change arms (fig 2-56). In its simplest form, movement of the collective pitch control causes the stationary and rotating stars, mounted centrally on the rotor shaft, to rise and descend. Movement of the cyclic pitch control causes the stars to tilt, the direction of tilt being controlled by the direction in which the cyclic stick is moved (fig 2-57).

transmitted to the rotor blade through pitch change arms. As the pitch change arms move up and down with each rotation of the star, blade pitch is constantly

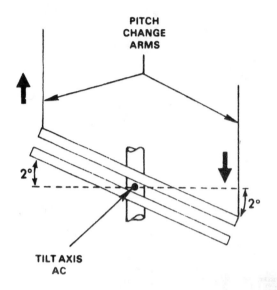

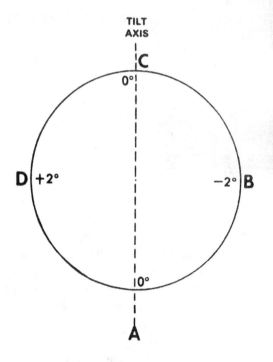

FIGURE 2-58. STATIONARY AND ROTATING STARS TILTED IN RELATION TO MAST.

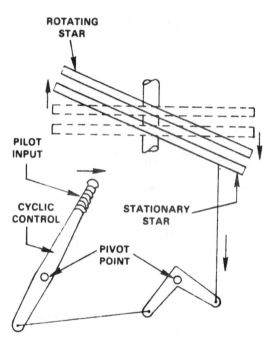

FIGURE 2-57. STATIONARY AND ROTATING STARS TILTED BY CYCLIC CONTROL.

Figure 2-58 illustrates a star that is tilted 2°. Notice the amount the star has been tilted at four positions, A, B, C and D. Points A and C form the axis about which the tilt occurs. At that axis the star remains at zero degrees. When the star is moved, the resulting motion change is

increased or decreased. If cyclic control is applied to tilt the rotor, the addition of collective pitch does not change the tilt of the star and rotor. It simply moves the star upward, so pitch is increased an equal amount on all blades simultaneously.

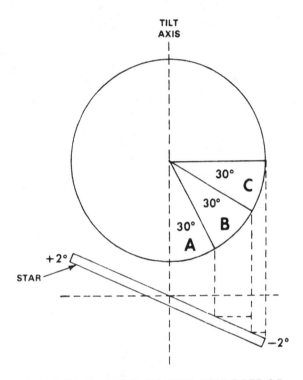

FIGURE 2-59. PITCH CHANGE ARM RATE OF MOVEMENT OVER 90° OF TRAVEL.

Figure 2-59 further illustrates how the pitch change arms move up and down on the tilted star. Rate of vertical change throughout the rotation is not uniform. Vertical movement is larger during the 30° of rotation at A than at B and C, respectively. This variation is repeated during each 90° of rotation. Rate of vertical movement is lowest at the low and high points of the star. Highest rates of vertical movement occur when the pitch change arms pass by the tilt axis of the star.

By means of cyclic pitch change, the rotor blades are caused to climb from point A to point B and then dive from point B to point A (fig 2-60). The rotor is tilted in the direction of desired flight in this way. In order for the blades to pass through points A and B, as shown in figure 2-60, it is obvious they must flap up and down on a hinge or teeter on a trunnion. When the blades are at the lowest flapping point (A, fig 2-60), it would appear that they would also be at their lowest pitch angle; and that at point B where they are at their highest flapping point, they would be at their highest pitch. If only aerodynamic considerations were involved this might be true. Because of phase lag, these points are separated by 90°.

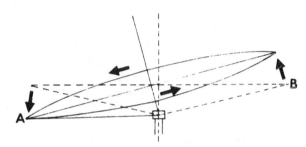

FIGURE 2-60. ROTOR FLAPPING IN RESPONSE TO CYCLIC INPUT.

☐ *Phase Lag.* In fact, the points of highest and lowest flapping are located 90° in the direction of rotation from the points of highest and lowest blade pitch. This phenomenon is called *phase lag*. The rotor control system is designed to correct for it, so the pilot is able to tilt the rotor disk in any direction by simply moving the cyclic control in that same direction.

Figure 2-61 illustrates a typical design feature that offsets cyclic control input 90°

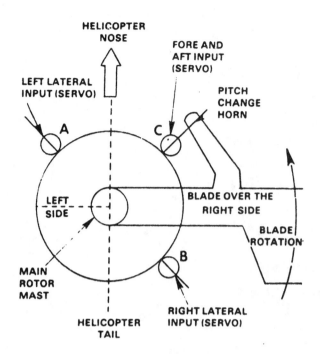

LEFT LATERAL
INPUT (SERVO)

HELICOPTER
NOSE

FORE AND
AFT INPUT
(SERVO)

PITCH
CHANGE
HORN

A

C

LEFT
SIDE

BLADE OVER THE
RIGHT SIDE

BLADE
ROTATION

MAIN
ROTOR
MAST

B

HELICOPTER
TAIL

RIGHT LATERAL
INPUT (SERVO)

FIGURE 2-61. INPUT SERVO AND PITCH
HORN OFFSET.

from where rotor tilt is desired. Rotor control input locations are the left lateral servo (A), right lateral servo (B), and the fore and aft servo (C). Note that each servo is offset 45° from the position corresponding to its name. For example, the fore and aft input servo is not located at the nose or tail position; instead, it is at the right front about halfway between the nose and the 3 o'clock position. Similarly, the left lateral servo is located halfway between the nose and the 9 o'clock position. The right lateral servo is stationed halfway between the tail and the 3 o'clock position. Location of the input servos accounts for part of the offset that is needed to correct for phase lag. Note also that the rotor blade has a pitch change horn that extends ahead of the blade in the plane of rotation about 45°. Pilot control inputs are transmitted from the input servos to the pitch change horn by a connecting rod called a pitch change rod.

Design of the pitch change horn, coupled with servo placement, provides the total offset necessary to compensate for phase lag.

Figure 2-62 illustrates typical cyclic pitch variation for a blade through one revolution with the cyclic pitch control full forward. Degree figures shown are for a typical aircraft rotor system and would vary depending on the type helicopter. Note that the input servos and pitch change horns are offset as described in the previous paragraph. With the cyclic pitch control in the full forward position, blade pitch angle is highest at the 9 o'clock position and lowest at the 3 o'clock position. Pitch angle begins decreasing as it passes 9 o'clock and decreases continually until it reaches the 3 o'clock position. As the blade moves forward from 3 o'clock, pitch begins to increase and reaches maximum pitch angle at 9 o'clock. Blade pitch angles over the nose and tail are about equal.

The blades reach a point of lowest flapping over the nose 90° in the direction of rotation from the point of lowest pitch angle (fig 2-62). Highest flapping occurs over the tail, 90° in the direction of rotation from the point of highest pitch angle. Simply stated, the force (pitch change) which causes blade flap must be applied to the blade 90° of rotation preceding the point where maximum blade flap is desired.

Patterns similar to figure 2-60 could be constructed for other cyclic positions in the circle of cyclic travel. In each case, the same principles apply. Points of highest and lowest flapping will be located 90° in the direction of rotation from the points of highest and lowest blade pitch.

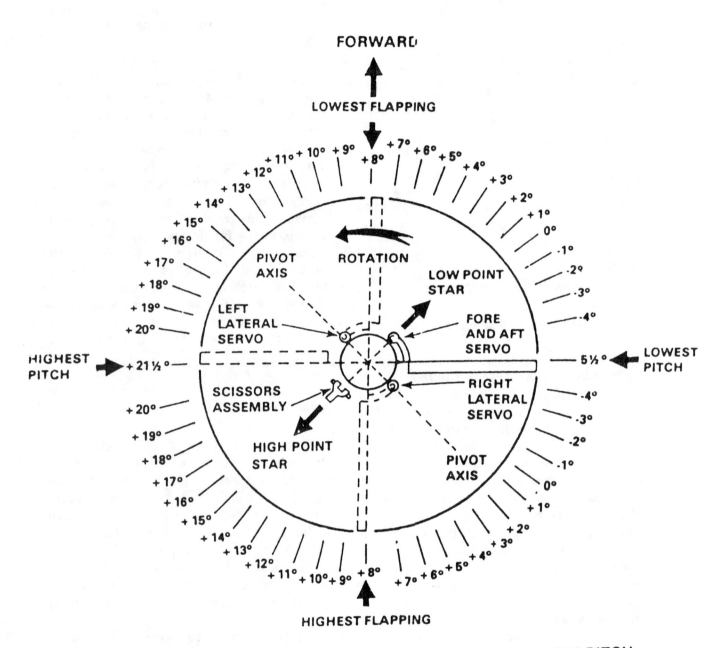

FIGURE 2-62. CYCLIC PITCH VARIATION—FULL FORWARD, LOW PITCH.

RETREATING BLADE STALL

☐ *Stall Tendency*. A tendency for the retreating blade to stall in forward flight is inherent in all present-day helicopters, and is a major factor in limiting their forward speed. Just as the stall of an airplane wing limits the low speed possibilities of the airplane, the stall of a rotor blade limits the high speed potential of a helicopter (fig 2-63). The airspeed of the retreating blade (the blade moving away from the direction of flight) slows down as forward speed increases. The retreating blade must, however, produce an amount of lift equal to that of the advancing blade (B, fig 2-63). Therefore, as the airspeed of the retreating blade decreases with forward speed, the blade angle of attack must be increased to equalize lift throughout the rotor disk area. As this angle increase is continued, the blade will stall at some high forward speed (C, fig 2-63).

As forward airspeed increases, the "no lift" areas (fig 2-63) move left of center, covering more of the retreating blade sectors. This requires more lift at the outer retreating blade portions to compensate for the loss of lift of the inboard retreating sections. In the area of reversed flow, the rotational velocity of this blade section is slower than the aircraft airspeed; therefore, the air flows from the trailing to leading edge of the airfoil. In the negative stall area, the rotational velocity of the airfoil is faster than the aircraft airspeed; therefore, air flows from leading to trailing edge of the blade. However due to the relative arm and induced flow, blade flapping is not sufficient to produce a positive angle of attack. Blade flapping and rotational velocity in the negative lift area are sufficient to produce a positive angle of attack, but not to a degree that produces appreciable lift.

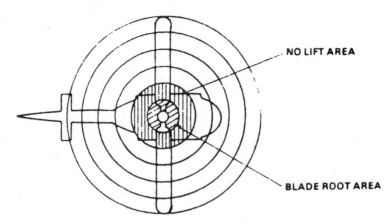

NO LIFT AREA

BLADE ROOT AREA

A. HOVERING LIFT PATTERN

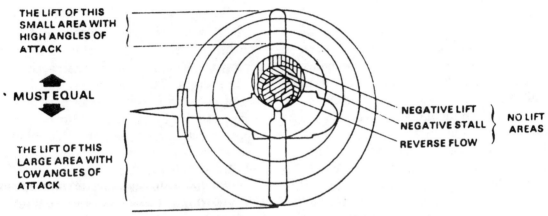

THE LIFT OF THIS SMALL AREA WITH HIGH ANGLES OF ATTACK

MUST EQUAL

THE LIFT OF THIS LARGE AREA WITH LOW ANGLES OF ATTACK

NEGATIVE LIFT
NEGATIVE STALL
REVERSE FLOW

NO LIFT AREAS

B. NORMAL CRUISE LIFT PATTERN

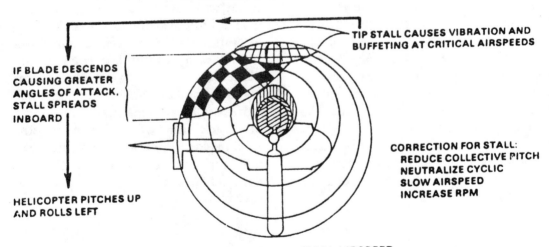

TIP STALL CAUSES VIBRATION AND BUFFETING AT CRITICAL AIRSPEEDS

IF BLADE DESCENDS CAUSING GREATER ANGLES OF ATTACK, STALL SPREADS INBOARD

HELICOPTER PITCHES UP AND ROLLS LEFT

CORRECTION FOR STALL:
REDUCE COLLECTIVE PITCH
NEUTRALIZE CYCLIC
SLOW AIRSPEED
INCREASE RPM

C. LIFT PATTERN AT CRITICAL AIRSPEED

FIGURE 2-63. RETREATING BLADE STALL.

Figure 2-64 shows a rotor disk that has reached a stall condition on the retreating side. It is assumed that the stall angle of attack for this rotor system is 14°. Distribution of angle of attack along the blade is shown at eight positions in the rotor disk. Although the blades are twisted and have less pitch at the tip than at the root, angle of attack is higher at the tip because of induced airflow.

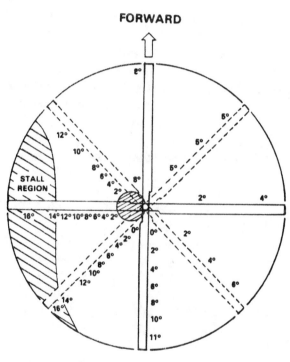

FORWARD

FIGURE 2-64. ANGLE OF ATTACK DISTRIBUTION DURING RETREATING BLADE STALL.

☐ *Effects*. Upon entry into blade stall, the first effect is generally a noticeable vibration of the helicopter. This is followed by a rolling tendency and a tendency for the nose to pitch up. The tendency to pitch up may be relatively insignificant for helicopters with semirigid rotor systems due to pendular action. If the cyclic stick is held forward and collective pitch is not reduced or is increased, this condition becomes aggravated; the vibration greatly increases, and control may be lost. By being familiar with the conditions which lead to blade stall, the aviator should realize when he is flying under such circumstances and should take corrective action.

The major warnings of approaching retreating blade stall conditions are—

● Abnormal vibration.

● Pitchup of the nose.

● Tendency for the helicopter to roll in the direction of the stalled side.

When operating at high forward speeds, the following conditions are most likely to produce blade stall:

● High blade loading (high gross weight).

● Low rotor RPM.

● High density altitude.

● Steep or abrupt turns.

● Turbulent air.

☐ *Corrective Actions*. When flight conditions are such that blade stall is likely, extreme caution should be exercised when maneuvering. An abrupt maneuver such as a steep turn or pullup may result in dangerously severe blade stall. Aircraft control and structural limitations of the helicopter would be threatened.

Blade stall normally occurs when airspeed is high. To prevent blade stall, the pilot must fly slower than normal when—

●The density altitude is much higher than standard.

●Carrying maximum gross loads.

●Flying high drag configurations, floats, external stores, weapons, speakers, floodlights, sling loads, etc.

●The air is turbulent.

When the pilot suspects blade stall, he can possibly prevent its occurrence by sequentially—

●Reducing power.

●Reducing airspeed.

●Reducing "G" loading during maneuvering.

●Increasing RPM toward upper limit.
●
Checking pedal trim.

In severe blade stall, the pilot loses control. The helicopter will pitch up violently and roll to the left. The only corrective action, then, is to accomplish procedures as indicated previously to shorten the duration of the stall and regain control.

COMPRESSIBLE FLOW

As helicopter speeds increase and missions become more varied, the helicopter pilot must learn to cope with the effects of compressibility encountered in high speed airflow. Earlier we described the qualities of incompressible airflow and said at low speeds it was analogous to the flow of water, hydraulic fluid, or any other incompressible fluid. It is this way because at low speeds air experiences relatively small changes in pressure with only *negligible* changes in *density*. However, at high speeds, the pressure changes that take place are larger and result in significant *air density* changes. The study of airflow at high speeds must account for these changes in *air density*. It must also consider that the air is compressible and that there will be compressibility effects.

The dominating factor in high speed airflow is the *speed of sound*. Speed of sound is the rate at which small pressure disturbances will be propagated through the air and this propagation speed is solely a function of air temperature. Figure 2-65 shows the variation of the speed of sound in the standard atmosphere.

ALTITUDE	TEMPERATURE		SPEED OF SOUND
Feet	°F	°C	Knots
Sea Level	59.0	15.0	661.7
5,000	41.2	5.1	650.3
10,000	23.3	-4.8	638.6
15,000	5.5	-14.7	626.7
20,000	-12.3	-24.6	614.6
25,000	-30.2	-34.5	602.2
30,000	-48.0	-44.4	589.6
35,000	-65.8	-54.3	576.6
40,000	-69.7	-56.5	573.8
50,000	-69.7	-56.5	573.8
60,000	-69.7	-56.5	573.8

FIGURE 2-65. VARIATION OF TEMPERATURE AND SPEED OF SOUND WITH ALTITUDE.

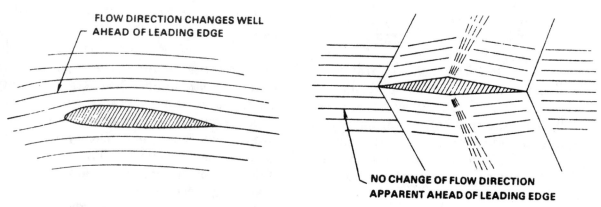

SUBSONIC FLOW PATTERN

FLOW DIRECTION CHANGES WELL
AHEAD OF LEADING EDGE

SUPERSONIC FLOW PATTERN

NO CHANGE OF FLOW DIRECTION
APPARENT AHEAD OF LEADING EDGE

FIGURE 2-66. COMPARISON OF SUBSONIC AND SUPERSONIC FLOW PATTERNS.

If the airfoil is traveling at some speed above the speed of sound, the airflow ahead of it will not be influenced by the pressure field, because pressure disturbances cannot be propagated ahead of the airfoil. Thus, as the speed nears the speed of sound, a compression wave forms at the leading edge and all changes in velocity and pressure take place sharply and suddenly. The airflow ahead of the airfoil is not influenced until the air particles are suddenly forced out of the way by the concentrated pressure wave set up by the airfoil. A typical supersonic airflow is shown in figure 2-66.

As an airfoil moves through the air, velocity and pressure changes occur which create pressure changes in the airflow surrounding the airfoil. These pressure changes are propagated through the air at the speed of sound. If the airfoil is traveling at low speed, the pressure disturbances are propagated ahead of it. The airflow immediately ahead of the airfoil is influenced by the pressure field on the airfoil. Evidence of how this pressure field influences the flow ahead of an airfoil

traveling at low speed is shown in figure 2-66.

It should become apparent that all compressibility effects depend upon the relationship of blade airspeed to the speed of sound. The term used to describe this relationship is the Mach number (M). This term is the relationship of the true airspeed to the speed of sound.

$$M = \frac{V}{a}$$

where: M = Mach number

V = true airspeed, knots

a = speed of sound, knots

= $a_0 \sqrt{\theta}$

a_0 = speed of sound at 288°K (15°C) is 661.7 knots

θ = temperature ratio

= T/T_0

Compressibility effects are not limited to speeds at and above the speed of sound. The aerodynamic shape of an airfoil causes local flow velocities which are greater than the blade speed. Thus, a blade can experience compressibility effects at speeds well below the speed of sound. Since there is the possibility of having *both* subsonic and supersonic flows existing on a blade, it is necessary to define certain regimes of flight as follows:

Subsonic - Mach numbers below 0.75

Transonic - Mach numbers from 0.75 to 1.20.

Supersonic - Mach numbers from 1.20 to 5.00

Although the Mach numbers used to define these regimes of flight are approximate, it is important to appreciate the types of flow existing in each area. In the subsonic regime, it is likely that pure subsonic airflow exists on all parts of the blade. In the transonic regime, it is very probable that flow on the blades may be partly subsonic and partly supersonic.

The principal differences between subsonic and supersonic flow are due to the *compressibility* of the supersonic flow. Figure 2-67 shows a comparison of incompressible and compressible flow through a closed tube. In both cases, assume the mass flow at any station along the tube is constant.

The example of subsonic incompressible flow is simplified by the fact that the *density* of flow is constant throughout the tube. As the flow approaches a constriction and the streamlines converge, velocity increases as static pressure decreases. In other words, a convergence of the tube requires an increasing velocity to accommodate the continuity of flow. Also, as the subsonic incompressible flow enters a diverging section of the tube, velocity decreases and static pressure increases while density remains unchanged. The behavior of subsonic incompressible flow is that a convergence causes expansion (decreasing pressure), while a divergence causes compression (increasing pressure).

The example of supersonic compressible flow is complicated by the fact that the variations of flow density are related to the changes in velocity and static pressure. The behavior of supersonic compressible flow is that a convergence causes compression, while a divergence causes expansion. Thus, as the supersonic compressible flow approaches a constriction and the streamlines converge, velocity decreases and static pressure increases. Continuity of mass flow is maintained by the increase in flow *density* which accompanies the decrease in velocity. As the supersonic compressible flow enters a diverging section of the tube, velocity increases, static pressure decreases, and density decreases to accommodate the condition of continuity.

Three significant differences emerge from the comparison between supersonic compressible and subsonic incompressible flow.

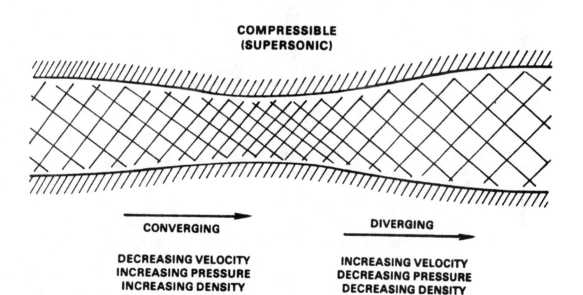

**INCOMPRESSIBLE
(SUBSONIC)**

CONVERGING

DIVERGING

INCREASING VELOCITY
DECREASING PRESSURE
CONSTANT DENSITY

DECREASING VELOCITY
INCREASING PRESSURE
CONSTANT DENSITY

**COMPRESSIBLE
(SUPERSONIC)**

CONVERGING

DIVERGING

DECREASING VELOCITY
INCREASING PRESSURE
INCREASING DENSITY

INCREASING VELOCITY
DECREASING PRESSURE
DECREASING DENSITY

**FIGURE 2-67. COMPARISON OF COMPRESSIBLE AND INCOMPRESSIBLE FLOW
THROUGH A CLOSED TUBE.**

☐ Compressible flow includes the additional variable of flow density.

☐ Convergence of flow causes expansion of incompressible flow, but compression of compressible flow.

☐ Divergence of flow causes compression of incompressible flow, but expansion of compressible flow.

An airfoil in subsonic flight which is producing lift will have local velocities on the surface which are greater than the free stream velocity. Hence, compressibility effects can be expected to occur at flight speeds less than the speed of sound. The transonic regime of flight provides the opportunity for mixed subsonic and supersonic flow and accounts for the first significant effects of compressibility.

Consider the conventional airfoil shape shown in figure 2-68. If this airfoil is at a flight Mach number of 0.50 and a slight positive angle of attack the maximum local velocity on the surface will be greater than the blade speed, but most likely less than sonic speed. Assume that an increase in blade Mach number to 0.72 would produce first evidence of local sonic flow. This condition of flight is the highest blade speed possible without supersonic flow, and is termed the *critical* Mach number. By definition, critical Mach number is the free stream Mach number which produces first evidence of local sonic flow. Therefore, shock waves, buffet, and airflow separation take place above critical Mach number.

As critical Mach number is exceeded, an area of supersonic airflow is created and a normal shock wave forms as the boundary between the supersonic flow and the subsonic flow on the aft portion of the airfoil surface. The acceleration of the airflow from subsonic to supersonic is smooth and without shock waves if the surface is smooth and the transition gradual. However, the transition of airflow from supersonic to subsonic is always accompanied by a shock wave. When there is no change in direction of the airflow, the wave form is a normal shock wave.

The normal shock wave is detached from the leading edge of the airfoil and is perpendicular to the upstream flow. The flow immediately behind the wave is subsonic. Figure 2-69 illustrates how an airfoil at high subsonic speeds has local flow velocities which are supersonic. As the local supersonic flow moves aft, a normal shock wave forms, slowing the flow to subsonic. A supersonic airstream passing through a *normal* shock wave will experience these changes:

☐ The airstream is slowed to subsonic; the local Mach number behind the wave is about equal to the reciprocal of the Mach number ahead of the wave—e.g., if Mach number ahead of the wave is 1.25, the Mach number of the flow behind the wave is approximately 0.80.

☐ The airflow direction immediately behind the wave is unchanged.

☐ The static pressure of the airstream behind the wave is increased greatly.

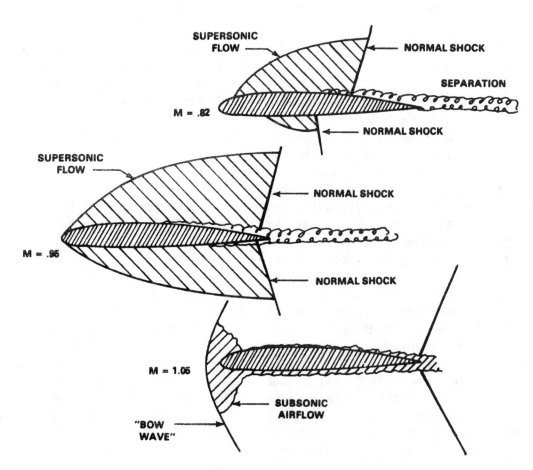

FIGURE 2-68. TRANSONIC FLOW PATTERNS.

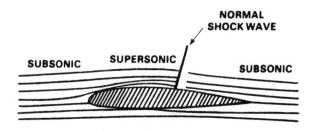

FIGURE 2-69. NORMAL SHOCK WAVE FORMATION.

☐ The density of the airstream behind the wave is increased greatly.

☐ The energy of the airstream indicated by total pressure is greatly reduced (dynamic plus static). The normal shock wave is very wasteful of energy.

As stated in the preceding paragraph, one of the principal effects of the normal shock wave is to produce a large increase in the static pressure of the airstream behind the wave. If the shock wave is strong, the boundary layer may separate. At speeds only slightly beyond critical Mach number, the shock wave formed is not strong enough to cause separation or any noticeable change in aerodynamic forces. However, a larger increase in speed above critical Mach number sufficient to form a strong shock wave can cause separation of the boundary layer and produce sudden changes in aerodynamic forces. Such a flow condition is shown in figure 2-68 by the flow pattern for $M = 0.77$. Notice a further increase in Mach number to 0.82 enlarges the supersonic area on the upper surface and forms an additional area of supersonic flow and normal shock wave on the lower surface.

As the blade speed approaches the speed of sound, the areas of supersonic flow enlarge and the shock waves move nearer the trailing edge (fig 2-68, $M = 0.95$). The boundary layer may remain separated or may reattach, depending upon airfoil shape and angle of attack. When the blade speed exceeds the speed of sound the "bow" wave forms at the leading edge. This typical flow pattern is shown in figure 2-68 by the drawing for $M = 1.05$. If speed is increased to some higher supersonic value, all oblique portions of the waves incline more greatly; and the detached normal shock portion of the bow wave moves closer to the leading edge.

Airflow separation induced by shock wave formation can create significant variations in aerodynamic force coefficients of the airfoil section. When the blade speed exceeds the critical Mach number some typical effects on an airfoil section are:

☐ An increase in the section drag coefficient for a given section lift coefficient.

☐ A decrease in section lift coefficient for a given section angle of attack.

☐ A change in section pitching moment coefficient. A comparison of drag coefficient versus Mach number for a constant lift coefficient is shown in figure 2-70. Note the sharp increase in the drag coefficient. This point is termed the "force divergence" Mach number and usually exceeds the critical Mach number by about 5 to 10 percent.

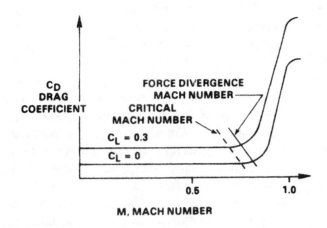

FIGURE 2-70. COMPRESSIBILITY DRAG RISE.

Since the speed of the helicopter is added to the speed of rotation of the advancing blade, the highest relative velocities occur at the tip of the advancing blade. When the Mach number of the tip section of the advancing blade exceeds the critical Mach number for the rotor blade section, compressibility effects result. The principal effects of compressibility are the large increase in drag and the rearward shift of the airfoil aerodynamic center. Compressibility effects on the helicopter increase the power required to maintain rotor RPM and cause rotor roughness, vibration, cyclic shake, and an undersirable structural twisting of the blade.

Compressibility effects become more severe at higher lift coefficients (higher blade angles of attack) and higher Mach numbers. The following operating conditions represent the most adverse compressibility conditions:

☐ High airspeed.

☐ High rotor RPM.

☐ High gross weight.

☐ High density altitude.

☐ Low temperature. The speed of sound is proportional to the square root of the absolute temperature. Therefore, sonic velocity will be more easily obtained at low temperatures when the sonic speed is lower.

☐ Turbulent air. Sharp gusts momentarily increase the blade angle of attack and thus lower the critical Mach number to the point where compressibility effects may be encountered on the blade.

Compressibility effects will vanish if blade pitch is decreased. The similarities in the critical conditions for retreating blade stall and compressibility should be noticed, but one basic difference must be appreciated. Compressibility occurs at high RPM while retreating blade stall occurs at low RPM. With the exception of RPM control, recovery technique is identical for both.

BLADE LEAD AND LAG

Fully articulated rotors have hinged blades that are free to move fore and aft in the plane of rotation independent of the other blades in the system. Movement about the hinge avoids bending stresses and is dampened by a drag damper to avoid undersirable oscillations. When the helicopter moves horizontally, the blade pitch angle continually changes throughout each revolution of the rotor to overcome dissymmetry of lift. Pitch angle variation causes changes in blade drag which makes the blade lead or lag about the drag hinge.

Another force, called *Coriolis force*, causes blades to lead and lag. Coriolis was a French mathematician who made a study of motion in a plane of rotation caused by periodic mass forces. This type of motion is governed by the law of conservation of angular momentum. The law states that a rotating body will continue to rotate with the same rotational velocity until some external force is applied to change the speed of rotation. Changes in angular velocity (angular acceleration or deceleration) will take place if the mass of a rotating body is moved closer to, or further from, the axis of rotation. If the mass is moved closer to the axis of rotation, the mass will accelerate. If the mass is moved away from the axis of rotation, it will decelerate. A common example that illustrates this law is the ice skater performing a rotating movement. The skater begins rotating on one foot with both arms and one leg extended out from the body. Rotation is relatively slow until the skater moves both arms and the leg in close to the body (axis of rotation). Suddenly rotational speed increases dramatically because the skater's center of mass has moved closer to the axis of rotation. Mass did not change and no external force was applied, so velocity had to increase.

Applying the principle of Coriolis force to a rotating helicopter blade, it may be stated:

☐ A mass moving radially outward on a rotating disk will exert a force opposite to rotation (deceleration).

☐ A mass moving radially inward on a rotating disk will exert a force in the direction of rotation (acceleration).

Consider the helicopter stationary on the ground in a no-wind condition with the rotor turning. The distance from the blade center of gravity to the shaft axis is constant throughout a complete blade revolution (a, b, fig 2-71). If the cyclic stick is moved laterally, the rotor blade will climb on one side of the disk and descend on the other side to produce a changed disk attitude. Since the helicopter is stationary on the ground, the shaft axis about which the blades are turning has not moved. The distance from the blade center of gravity to the shaft axis changes continuously through each 360° of travel (c, d, fig 2-71). On the side where the blade climbs, the radius (d, fig 2-71) decreases and the blade accelerates (leads). The opposite side has a descending blade and an increasing radius (c, fig 2-71), causing the blade to decelerate (lag).

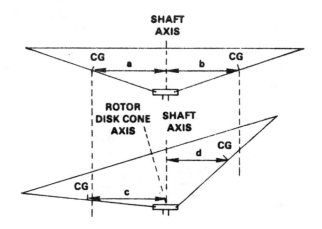

FIGURE 2-71. RADIUS CHANGE OF BLADE CG RELATIVE TO DISK ATTITUDE.

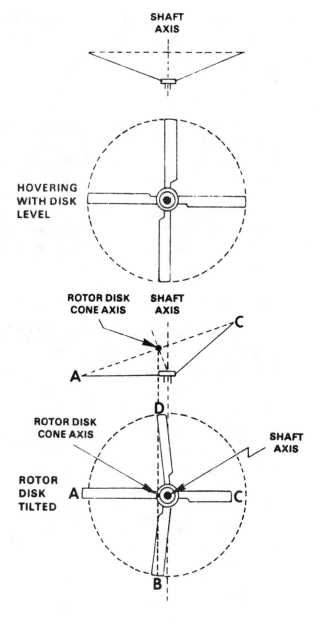

FIGURE 2-72. LEAD AND LAG.

has descended and begins to decelerate. As it decelerates, it lags enough to aline with the rotor disk cone axis at point B. At point C the blade has climbed which decreases the distance from center of gravity (*CG*) to shaft axis resulting in an acceleration force. At D the blade is leading as a result of acceleration and has moved ahead to aline with the cone axis. This phenomenon occurs whenever the shaft axis and cone axis are separated by a tilted rotor disk.

CYCLIC CONTROL STICK POSITION VERSUS AIRSPEED RELATIONSHIP

The cyclic control stick plot (fig 2-73) is an engineering graph made by a stylus placed on the cyclic stick. This permits a graphic plot and a record of stick positions required to maintain various steady-state airspeeds. The stick plot may cover the entire flight envelope, starting from the

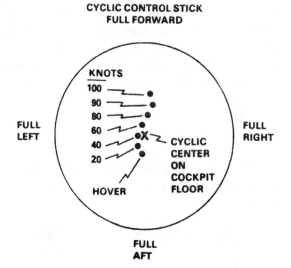

CYCLIC CONTROL STICK PLOT (TYPICAL)

FIGURE 2-73. CYCLIC CENTER OF CONTROL SHIFT.

Figure 2-72 illustrates lead and lag of a four-bladed rotor, using a side view and a top view of the rotor system. Note that the blades are evenly spaced 90° apart on the level disk. The tilted rotor disk has uneven spacing between the blades because of lead and lag. At point A, figure 2-72, the blade

hover and continuing on to "velocity never exceed" (*Vne*) airspeeds, and perhaps blade stall. The stick plot was originally used to record cyclic travel for initial certification of newly designed or extensively modified helicopters.

The cyclic stick action required by the aviator for control of attitude, for changing attitudes, and for the prevention and correction of dissymmetry of lift is as follows:

☐ The pilot applies slight cyclic control stick pressures and counterpressures around the hover cyclic center to maintain the hover and to correct deviations of the rotor from the level attitude.

☐ The pilot applies slight pressures and counterpressures while rotating to an acceleration attitude; then additional slight corrections are made to hold the acceleration attitude constant.

☐ As the airspeed approaches the next higher speed zone (each 10 to 15 knots), the pilot must reposition the cyclic stick further forward as the center of control shifts (brought about by the correction required for dissymmetry of lift, fig 2-73).

☐ At any forward steady-state airspeed (e.g., 80 knots), the pilot must use constant slight corrective pressures around the 80-knot cyclic center to hold the specific attitude for 80 knots.

☐ If the pilot applies a slight aft cyclic stick to assume a deceleration attitude, the cyclic stick returns to the 80-knot setting. Then the aviator applies corrective pressures to hold the deceleration attitude constant.

☐ To hold the same decelerating attitude as the airspeed actually reduces (e.g., to 60 knots), the pilot must reposition his center of control rearward as shown in figure 2-73.

☐ During a flight from the hover to *Vne* values and back to termination of flight at a hover, the cyclic control center shifts as airspeed is changed. Therefore, the pilot should be more aware of the specific attitude as the real measure of control, rather than place any overdependence on the methods based upon feel, touch, and/or coordination.

EFFECT OF ROTOR SYSTEM DESIGN ON WEIGHT AND BALANCE LIMITATIONS

Weight and balance limitations change greatly with different main rotor system configurations.

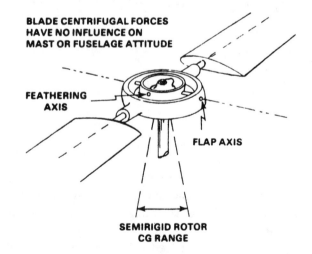

BLADE CENTRIFUGAL FORCES HAVE NO INFLUENCE ON MAST OR FUSELAGE ATTITUDE

FEATHERING AXIS

FLAP AXIS

SEMIRIGID ROTOR CG RANGE

FIGURE 2-74. SEMIRIGID ROTOR SYSTEM.

☐ A semirigid rotor system only supplies support and mobility to the free hanging pendulous mass of the fuselage (fig 2-74). Therefore, it has a limited allowance for center of gravity travel (fig 2-76).

☐ In a fully articulated rotor system with offset hinges (fig 2-75), blade centrifugal forces assist the fuselage to support a wide-range center of gravity travel (fig 2-76).

☐ A rigid (hingeless) rotor system provides rotor rigidity in which centrifugal blade forces hold the fuselage level throughout a very wide center of gravity tolerance laterally and fore and aft (fig 2-76).

☐ A multirotor system using differential collective has the greatest allowance for center of gravity travel (fig 2-76).

BLADE CENTRIFUGAL FORCES APPLIED TO OFFSET HINGES HAVE STRONG INFLUENCE ON MAST AND FUSELAGE ATTITUDE.

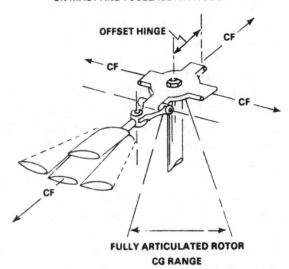

FULLY ARTICULATED ROTOR
CG RANGE

FIGURE 2-75. FULLY ARTICULATED ROTOR SYSTEM WITH OFFSET HINGES.

SEMIRIGID ROTOR

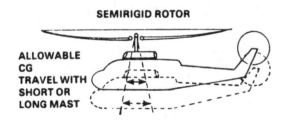

ALLOWABLE CG TRAVEL WITH SHORT OR LONG MAST

FULLY ARTICULATED ROTOR

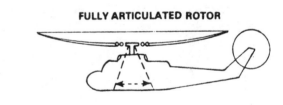

RIGID ROTOR

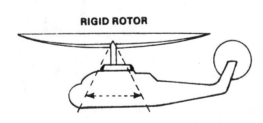

MULTIROTOR

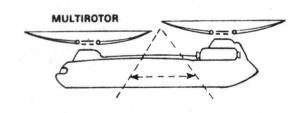

FIGURE 2-76. EFFECT OF ROTOR SYSTEM ON CENTER OF GRAVITY TRAVEL.

DANGER OF EXCEEDING CENTER OF GRAVITY LIMITS

The permissible center of gravity travel is very limited in many helicopters. The weight of the crew, fuel, passengers, cargo, etc., must be carefully distributed to prevent the helicopter from flying with a dangerous nose-low, nose-high, or lateral (side-low) attitude. If such *CG* attitudes exceed the limits of cyclic controls, the rotor will be forced to follow the tilt of the fuselage, and control may be lost.

The helicopter will then move at a speed and direction proportionate to the tilt of the rotor system. The amount of cyclic control the aviator can apply to level the rotor system could be limited by the manner in which the helicopter is loaded. If a helicopter is loaded "out of *CG* limits" (①, fig 2-77), the aviator may find that when he applies corrective cyclic control (②, fig 2-77) as far as it will go, the helicopter attitude will remain low in the direction *CG* limits are exceeded. He will not be able to level the helicopter to decelerate and land. This creates an extremely dangerous situation (③, fig 2-77).

In newer helicopter designs, efforts have been made to place the loading compartment directly under the main rotor mast to minimize *CG* travel effects. However, the aviator must still exercise care in loading, and arrange his load to assure that it is centered within allowable *CG* travel limits of his helicopter as prescribed in the Operator's Manual for the particular helicopter.

The final check for *CG* is made operationally just prior to the takeoff to a hover.

☐ In flight, a *CG* centered in the forward portion of the envelope will result in relatively nose-low attitudes.

☐ An aft *CG* condition will result in relatively nose-high flight attitudes.

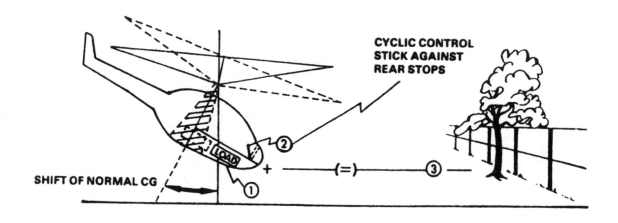

FIGURE 2-77. EXCESSIVE LOADING FORWARD OF THE CENTER OF GRAVITY.

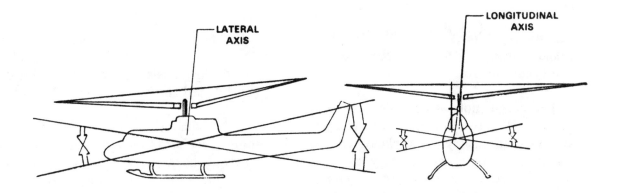

FIGURE 2-78. CYCLIC CONTROL RESPONSE AROUND THE LONGITUDINAL AXIS AND THE LATERAL AXIS.

☐ A lateral *CG* displacement will result in a relatively right-side or left-side low flight attitude. The correct procedure then is to cruise with one side low.

☐ A common error is to level the lateral *CG* attitude by use of a "forward-slip" (excess trim pedal). This causes a broadside wind and a lateral drag that levels the fuselage. This drag costs more power at cruise and results in less range. In autorotation, this fuselage drag would result in a greater rate of descent and a shortened gliding distance.

PENDULAR ACTION

Since the fuselage of the helicopter is suspended from a single point and has considerable mass, it is free to oscillate laterally or longitudinally in the same way as a pendulum.

☐ Normally, the fuselage follows the rules which govern pendulums, balance, and inertia.

☐ The rotor systems follow rules governing aerodynamics, dynamics, and gyroscopics.

☐ Fortunately, these two unrelated systems form a close and compatible partnership which normally avoids serious conflict.

Other factors which affect the relationship of the rotor system and fuselage are:

☐ *Overcontrolling.* Overcontrolling results when aviator cyclic control stick movements cause rotor tip changes that are not reflected in corresponding fuselage attitude changes. Correct aviator cyclic control movements (free of overcontrol) cause the rotor tip-path and the fuselage to move in unison.

Erratic airspeed and altitude control may not be due to overcontrolling, but may result from a lack of knowledge of attitude flying techniques.

☐ *Cyclic control response (single rotor helicopter).* The rotor's response to cyclic control input has no lag. The rotor blades respond instantly to the slightest touch of the cyclic control.

There is a noticeable difference in the fuselage response to lateral cyclic compared to fore and aft cyclic applications. Normally it requires considerably more fore and aft cyclic movement to achieve the same fuselage response as is achieved from an equal amount of lateral cyclic. This is not a lag in rotor response. It is due to more fuselage inertia around the lateral axis as compared to fuselage inertia around the longitudinal axis (fig 2-78). For semirigid helicopters, the normal corrective device is the addition of a synchronized elevator attached to the tail boom and operated by the cyclic stick. This elevator forces the fuselage to follow the rotor at normal flight airspeeds; however, it is ineffective at slow airspeeds.

☐ *Shift of attitude due to fuel expenditure.* Fuel cells normally have a slight aft *CG*. As fuel is used there is a slight shift to a more nose-low attitude.

Due to fuel expenditure and a lighter fuselage, cruise attitudes tend to shift slightly lower. As fuel loads are reduced, the lighter fuselage is affected more by drag which results in a more nose-down attitude. Therefore, there is a slight shift to a more nose-low attitude during the flight period.

FUSELAGE ADD-ONS, FIXES, AND MODIFICATIONS

Fuselage nose-low attitude at cruise is typical of the single rotor helicopter.

☐ The causes of this condition are—

● The fuselage attitude alining itself to the tilted rotor disk at cruise airspeeds.

● Helicopter propulsion thrust is applied horizontally from the aerodynamic center of the main rotor; therefore, the total flat plate drag of the fuselage (centered many feet below the rotor) will cause an additional nose-low influence.

☐ The usual corrective measures are—

● Mounting the transmission in the fuselage with some degree of forward tilt presets the rotor system at the cruise airspeed tilt angle, while providing a level fuselage at cruise airspeeds.

● Adding a horizontal stabilizer or synchronized elevator on the tail boom. This will counteract the fuselage drag by holding the tail down and the fuselage level in cruise flight.

Fuselage add-on devices, external stores, or sling loads all perform useful services during certain modes of flight. However, these add-on surfaces or devices often add flat plate drag and develop troublesome side effects at higher or lower airspeeds, or hovering in crosswind/downwind conditions. Fuselage add-on devices include—

☐ Airfoil-shaped tail rotor pylons.

☐ Fixed or controllable elevators.

☐ Fixed-wing panels (experimental).

☐ Ventral fins and vertical stabilizers.

☐ Spoilers.

☐ Amphibious gear or floats.

☐ Dust or spray rigs.

☐ External pods.

☐ External ordnance and related hardware.

☐ Guns, cameras, or floodlights.

☐ Sling loads.

Additional problems of the pendulous fuselage are—

☐ Weather vane effect in crosswind hovering.

☐ Very poor inherent pedal trim (fuselage often drags somewhat sideward in flight due to a lack of pilot assist trim device).

☐ The possibility of rotor blade strikes on the fuselage. Poorly controlled slope operations or run-on landings with hard jolting touchdowns and poor heading control cause unacceptable force moments (or fuselage attitudes) that exceed main rotor/fuselage compatibility. These impacts increase the possibility of rotor blade strikes on the tail boom or the ground.

SETTLING WITH POWER

Settling with power is a condition of powered flight where the helicopter settles in its own downwash. The condition may also be referred to as the *vortex ring state*.

Conditions conducive to settling with power are a vertical or near vertical descent of at least 300 feet per minute and low forward speed. The rotor system must also be using some of the available engine power (from 20 to 100 percent) with insufficient power available to retard the sink rate. These conditions occur during approaches with a tailwind or during formation approaches when some aircraft are flying in turbulence from other aircraft.

Under the conditions described above, the helicopter may descend at a high rate which exceeds the normal downward induced flow rate of the inner blade sections. As a result, the airflow of the inner blade sections is upward relative to the disk. This produces a *secondary* vortex ring in addition to the normal tip vortex system. The secondary vortex ring is generated about the point on the blade where airflow changes from up to down. The result is an unsteady turbulent flow over a large area of the disk which causes loss of rotor efficiency even though power is still supplied from the engine.

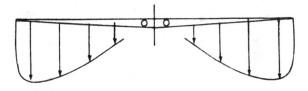

FIGURE 2-79. INDUCED FLOW VELOCITY DURING HOVERING FLIGHT.

Figure 2-79 shows the induced flow along the blade span during hovering flight. Downward velocity is highest at the blade tip where blade airspeed is highest. As blade airspeed decreases nearer the disk

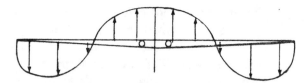

FIGURE 2-80. INDUCED FLOW VELOCITY DURING
VORTEX RING STATE.

center, downward velocity is less. Figure 2-80 shows the induced airflow velocity pattern along the blade span during a descent conducive to settling with power. The descent is so rapid that induced flow at the inner portion of the blades is upward rather than downward. The upflow caused by the descent has overcome the downflow produced by blade rotation. If the helicopter descends under these conditions, with insufficient power to slow or stop the descent, it will enter the vortex ring state (fig 2-81). During the vortex ring state, roughness and loss of control is experienced because of the turbulent rotational flow on the blades and the unsteady shifting of the flow along the blade span.

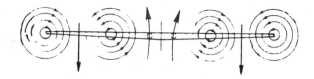

FIGURE 2-81. VORTEX RING STATE.

Figure 2-82 shows the relationship of horizontal speed versus vertical speed for a typical helicopter in a descent. Straight lines emanating from the upper left corner are lines of constant descent angle. Superimposed on this grid are flow state regions for the typical helicopter. From this illustration, several conclusions regarding the vortex ring state can be drawn.

☐ The vortex ring state can be completely avoided by descending on flightpaths shallower than about 30° (at any speed).

☐ For steeper approaches, vortex ring state can be avoided by using a speed either faster or slower than the area of severe turbulence and thrust variation.

☐ At very shallow angles of descent, the vortex ring wake is shed behind the helicopter.

☐ At steep angles, the vortex ring wake is below the helicopter at slow rates of descent and above the helicopter at high rates of descent.

Power settling is an unstable condition. If allowed to continue, the sink rate will reach sufficient proportions for the flow to be entirely up through the rotor system. If continued, the rate of descent will reach extremely high rates. Recovery may be initiated during the early stages of power settling by putting on a large amount of excess power. During the early stages of power settling, the large amount of excess power may be sufficient to overcome the upflow near the center of the rotor. If the sink rate reaches a higher rate, power will not be available to break this upflow and thus alter the vortex ring state of flow.

Normal tendency is for pilots to recover from a descent by application of collective pitch and power. If insufficient power is available for recovery, this action may aggravate power settling resulting in more turbulence and a higher rate of descent. Recovery can be accomplished by lowering collective pitch and increasing forward speed. Both of these methods of recovery require altitude to be successful.

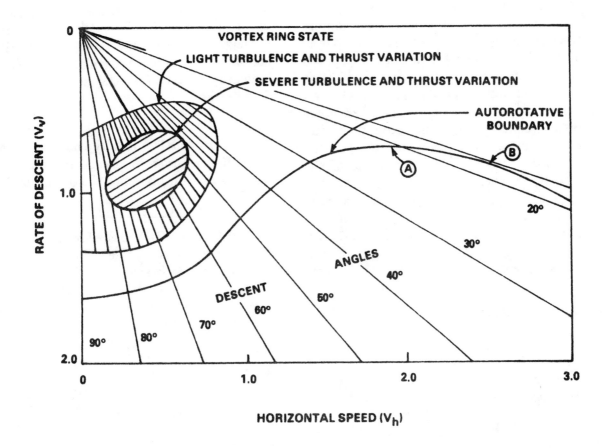

FIGURE 2-82. FLOW STATES IN DESCENDING FORWARD FLIGHT.

RESONANCE

Certain helicopter designs are subject to *sympathetic* and *ground resonance*.

☐ *Sympathetic resonance* is a harmonic beat between the main and tail rotor systems or other components or assemblies which might damage the helicopter. This type of resonance has been engineered out of most helicopters (e.g., by designing the main and tail gearboxes in odd decimal ratios). Thus, the beat of one component (assembly) cannot, under normal conditions, harmonize with the beat of another

component; and sympathetic resonance is not of immediate concern to the aviator. However, when resonance ranges are not designed out, the helicopter tachometer is appropriately marked; and the resonance range must be avoided (see applicable Operator's Manual).

☐ *Ground resonance* may develop in helicopters having fully articulated rotor systems when a series of shocks cause the rotor blades in the system to become positioned in unbalanced displacement. If this oscillating condition is allowed to progress, it can be self-energizing and extremely dangerous; and it usually results in structural failure. Ground resonance is most common to three-bladed helicopters having landing wheels. The rotor blades in a three-bladed helicopter are equally spaced (120°), but are constructed to allow some horizontal lead and lag action. Ground resonance occurs when the helicopter makes contact with the ground during landing or takeoff. When one wheel of the helicopter strikes the ground ahead of the other(s), a shock is transmitted through the fuselage to the rotor. Another shock is transmitted when the next wheel hits. The first shock from ground contact (A, fig 2-83) causes the blades straddling the contact point to jolt out of angular balance.

If repeated by the next contact (B, fig 2-83), a resonance is established which sets up a self-energizing oscillation of the fuselage. Unless immediate corrective action is taken, the oscillation severity increases rapidly and the helicopter may disintegrate.

•If rotor RPM is in the normal range, take off to a hover. A change of rotor RPM may also aid in breaking the oscillation.

• If rotor RPM is below the normal range, reduce power. Use of the rotor brake may also aid in breaking the oscillation.

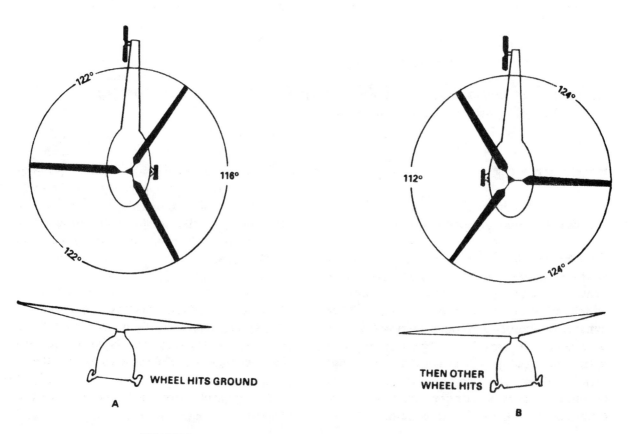

FIGURE 2-83. GROUND SHOCK CAUSING BLADE UNBALANCE.

AERODYNAMICS OF VERTICAL AUTOROTATION

During powered flight, the rotor drag is overcome with engine power. When the engine fails, or is deliberately disengaged from the rotor system, some other force must be used to sustain rotor RPM so controlled flight can be continued to the ground. This force is generated by adjusting the collective pitch to allow a controlled descent. Airflow during helicopter descent provides the energy to overcome blade drag and turn the rotor. When the helicopter is descending in this manner, it is said to be in a state of *autorotation*. In effect the pilot gives up altitude at a controlled rate in return for energy to turn the rotor at an RPM which provides aircraft control. Stated another way, the helicopter has potential energy by virtue of its position (altitude). As altitude decreases, potential energy is converted to kinetic energy and stored in the turning rotor. The pilot uses this kinetic energy to cushion the touchdown when near the ground.

Most autorotations are performed with forward speed. For simplicity, the following aerodynamic explanation is based on a vertical autorotative descent (no forward speed) in still air. Under these conditions, the forces that cause the blades to turn are similar for all blades regardless of their position in the plane of rotation. Dissymmetry of lift resulting from helicopter airspeed is therefore not a factor, but will be discussed later.

During vertical autorotation, the rotor disk is divided into three regions as illustrated in figure 2-84.

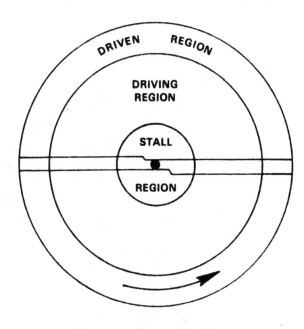

FIGURE 2-84. BLADE REGIONS IN VERTICAL AUTOROTATION DESCENT.

☐ The *driven region*, also called the *propeller region*, is nearest to the blade tips and normally consists of about 30 percent of the radius. The total aerodynamic force in this region is inclined slightly behind the rotating axis. This results in a drag force which tends to slow the rotation of the blade.

☐ The *driving region*, or *autorotative region*, normally lies between about 25 to 70 percent of the blade radius. Total aerodynamic force in this region is inclined slightly forward of the axis of rotation. This inclination supplies thrust which tends to accelerate the rotation of the blade.

☐ The *stall region* includes the inboard 25 percent of the blade radius. It operates above the stall angle of attack and causes drag which tends to slow the rotation of the blade.

Figure 2-85 shows three blade sections that illustrate force vectors in the driven region (A), a region of equilibrium (B), and the driving region (C). The force vectors are different in each region, because the rotational relative wind is slower near the blade root and increases continually toward the blade tip. When the inflow up through the rotor combines with rotational relative wind, it produces different combinations of aerodynamic force at every point along the blade.

In the driven region (A, fig 2-85), the total aerodynamic force acts behind the axis of rotation, resulting in an overall dragging force. This area produces lift; but it also opposes rotation and continually tends to decelerate the blade. The size of this region varies with blade pitch setting, rate of descent, and rotor RPM. When the pilot takes action to change autorotative RPM, blade pitch, or rate of descent, he is in effect changing the size of the driven region in relation to the other regions.

Between the driven region and the driving region is a point of equilibrium (B, fig 2-85). At this point on the blade, total aerodynamic force is alined with the axis of rotation. Lift and drag are produced, but the total effect produces neither acceleration nor deceleration. Point D is also an area of equilibrium in regard to thrust and drag.

Area C, figure 2-85, is the driving region of the blade and produces the forces needed to turn the blades during autorotation. Total aerodynamic force in the driving region is inclined forward of the axis of rotation and produces a continual acceleration force. Driving region size varies with blade pitch setting, rate of descent and rotor RPM. The pilot controls the size of this region in relation to the driven and stall regions in order to adjust autorotative RPM. For example, if the collective pitch stick is raised, the pitch angle will increase in all regions. This causes the point of equilibrium (B, fig 2-85) to move toward the blade tip, decreasing the size of the driven region. The entire driving region also moves toward the blade tip. The stall region becomes larger and the total blade drag is increased, causing RPM decrease.

A constant rotor RPM is achieved by adjusting the collective pitch stick so blade acceleration forces from the driving region (C, fig 2-85) are balanced with the deceleration forces from the driven and stall regions (A, E, fig 2-85).

AERODYNAMICS OF AUTOROTATION IN FORWARD FLIGHT

Autorotative force in forward flight is produced in exactly the same manner as when the helicopter is descending vertically in still air. However, because forward speed changes the inflow of air up through the rotor disk, the driving region and stall region move toward the retreating side of the disk where angle of attack is larger (fig 2-86). Because of lower angles of attack on the advancing side blade, more of that blade falls in the driven region. On the

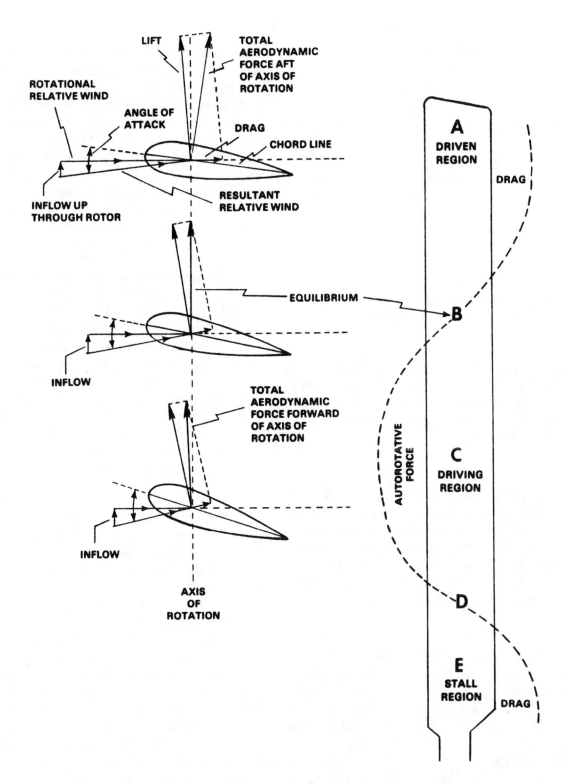

LIFT

TOTAL AERODYNAMIC FORCE AFT OF AXIS OF ROTATION

ROTATIONAL RELATIVE WIND

ANGLE OF ATTACK

DRAG

CHORD LINE

INFLOW UP THROUGH ROTOR

RESULTANT RELATIVE WIND

EQUILIBRIUM

INFLOW

TOTAL AERODYNAMIC FORCE FORWARD OF AXIS OF ROTATION

INFLOW

AXIS OF ROTATION

A
DRIVEN REGION

DRAG

B

AUTOROTATIVE FORCE

C
DRIVING REGION

D

E
STALL REGION

DRAG

FIGURE 2-85. FORCE VECTORS IN VERTICAL AUTOROTATIVE DESCENT.

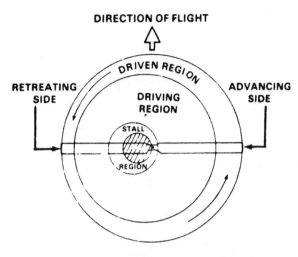

FIGURE 2-86. AUTOROTATIVE REGIONS IN FORWARD FLIGHT.

retreating side blade, more of the blade is in the stall region; and a small section near the root experiences a reversed flow. The size of the driven region on the retreating side is reduced.

Autorotations may be divided into three distinct phases: the *entry*, the *steady state descent*, and the *deceleration and touch-down*. Each of these phases is aerodynamically different than the others. The following discussion describes forces pertinent to each phase.

☐ *Entry* into autorotation is performed following loss of engine power. Immediate indications of power loss are rotor RPM decay and an out-of-trim condition. Rate of RPM decay is most rapid when the helicopter is at high gross weight, high forward speed, or in high density altitude conditions. All of these conditions demand increased collective pitch and torque to maintain powered flight and so result in

rapid RPM decay when the engine stops. In most helicopters, it takes only seconds for the RPM decay to reach a minimum safe range. Pilots must react quickly and initiate a reduction in collective pitch that will prevent excessive RPM decay. A cyclic flare will help prevent excessive decay if the failure occurs at high speed. This technique varies with the model helicopter. Pilots should consult and follow the appropriate aircraft Operator's Manual.

● Figure 2-87 shows the airflow and force vectors for a blade in powered flight at high speed. Note that the lift and drag vectors are large and the total aerodynamic force is inclined well to the rear of the axis of rotation. If the engine stops when the helicopter is in this condition, rotor RPM decay is rapid. To prevent RPM decay, the pilot must promptly lower the collective pitch control to reduce drag and incline the total aerodynamic force vector forward so it is near the axis of rotation.

● Figure 2-88 shows the airflow and force vectors for a helicopter just after power loss. The collective pitch has been reduced, but the helicopter has not started to descend. Note that lift and drag are reduced and the total aerodynamic force vector is inclined further forward than it was in powered flight. As the helicopter begins to descend, the airflow changes. This causes the total aerodynamic force to incline further forward. It will reach an equilibrium that maintains a safe operating RPM. The pilot establishes a glide at the proper airspeed which is 50 to 75 knots, depending on the helicopter and its gross weight. Rotor RPM should be stabilized at autorotative RPM which is normally a few turns higher than normal operating RPM.

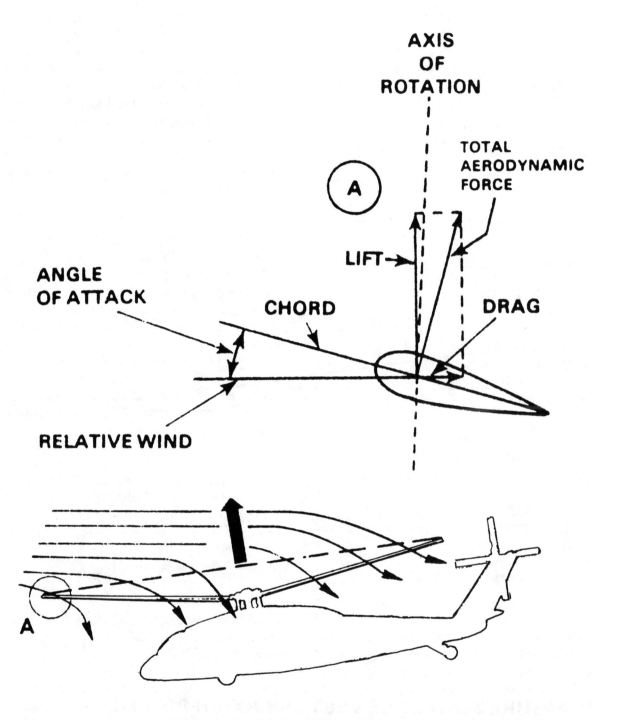

AXIS OF ROTATION

Ⓐ

TOTAL AERODYNAMIC FORCE

LIFT→

ANGLE OF ATTACK

CHORD

DRAG

RELATIVE WIND

FIGURE 2-87. FORCE VECTORS IN LEVEL POWERED FLIGHT AT HIGH SPEED.

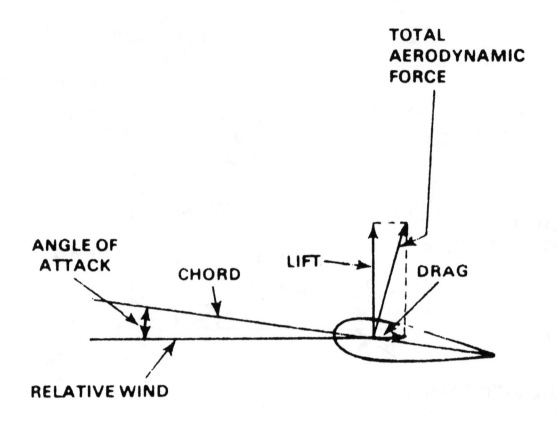

TOTAL AERODYNAMIC FORCE

ANGLE OF ATTACK

CHORD

LIFT

DRAG

RELATIVE WIND

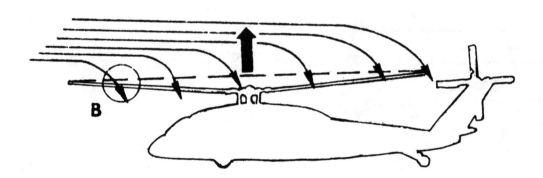

B

FIGURE 2-88. FORCE VECTORS AFTER POWER
LOSS WITH REDUCED COLLECTIVE.

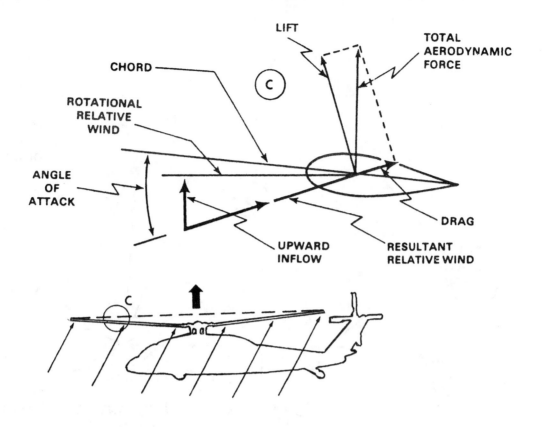

FIGURE 2-89. FORCE VECTORS IN AUTOROTATION STEADY STATE DESCENT.

☐ Figure 2-89 shows the helicopter in a *steady state descent*. Airflow is now upward through the rotor disk due to the descent. Changed airflow creates a larger angle of attack although blade pitch angle is the same as it was in figure 2-88 before the descent began. Total aerodynamic force is increased and inclined forward so equilibrium is established. Rate of descent and RPM are stabilized, and the helicopter is descending at a constant angle. Angle of descent is normally 17° to 20°, depending on airspeed, density altitude, wind, the model helicopter and other variables.

☐ Figure 2-90 illustrates the aerodynamics of autorotative *deceleration*. To successfully perform an autorotative landing, the pilot must reduce airspeed and rate of descent just before touchdown. Both of these actions can be partially accomplished by moving the cyclic control to the rear and changing the attitude of the rotor disk with relation to the relative wind (fig 2-90). The attitude change inclines the total force of the rotor disk to the rear and slows forward speed. It also increases angle of attack on all blades by changing the inflow of air. As a result, total rotor lifting force is increased and rate of descent is reduced. RPM also increases when the total aerodynamic force vector is lengthened (fig 2-90), thereby increasing blade kinetic energy available to cushion the touchdown. After forward speed is reduced to a safe landing speed, the helicopter is placed in a landing attitude as collective pitch is applied to cushion the touchdown. Specific values for RPM, airspeed, and technique are found in appropriate aircraft Operator's Manuals.

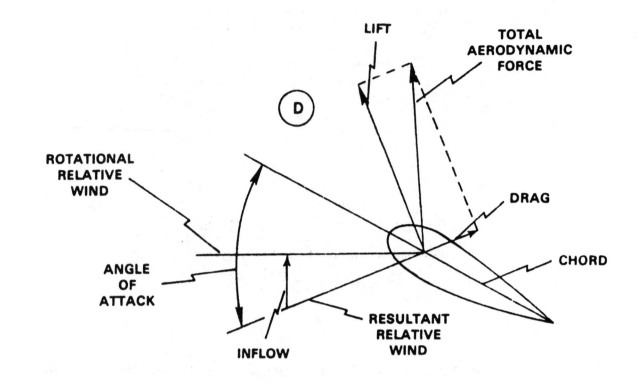

LIFT

TOTAL AERODYNAMIC FORCE

(D)

ROTATIONAL RELATIVE WIND

DRAG

CHORD

ANGLE OF ATTACK

INFLOW

RESULTANT RELATIVE WIND

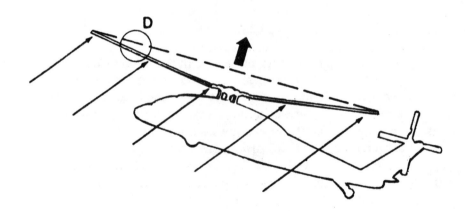

D

FIGURE 2-90. AUTOROTATIVE DECELERATION.

GLIDE AND RATE OF
DESCENT IN AUTOROTATION

Helicopter airspeed is probably the most significant factor affecting rate of descent in autorotation. Rate of descent is large at very low airspeeds; descreases to a minimum at some intermediate speed; then increases again at faster speed. Figure 2-82 shows the relationship between speed and rate of descent. Note that rate of descent is highest at zero horizontal speed. It decreases and reaches the minimum rate at point A, an intermediate horizontal speed. Then rate of descent increases again and provides the shallowest possible flightpath angle at point B, where the degree angle line is tangent to the autorotative boundary line. This is the best horizontal speed for maximum glide distance.

Each type helicopter has specific airspeeds (given in the autorotation chart of the Operator's Manual) at which a poweroff glide will cover maximum distance. This airspeed is usually at, or slightly above, normal cruise airspeed. Also shown in these charts are airspeeds which will result in the slowest rate of descent. These airspeeds usually are at, or near, slow cruise airspeed.

Specific airspeeds for maximum distance or slowest rate of descent are established on the basis of standard density altitude with average weather and wind conditions and normal loading. When the helicopter is operated with excessive loads in high density altitude or strong, gusty wind conditions, best performance is achieved from a slightly increased airspeed during the descent. For autorotation in light winds and low density altitude, best performance is achieved from a slight decrease in normal airspeed. Following this general procedure of fitting airspeed to existing conditions, an aviator can achieve approximately the same glide angle in any set of circumstances and estimate his touchdown point.

For example, the best glide ratio (maximum distance) for the average helicopter, in a no-wind condition, is about 4 feet of forward glide to 1 foot of descent. Ideal airspeed for minimum rate of descent is at slow cruise values and with a glide ratio of 3 feet forward to 1 foot of descent. Above and below this airspeed, the rate of descent rapidly increases.

A study of the autorotation chart in figure 2-91 shows typical rates of descent for the various airspeeds for steady state autorotation. This type of graph in an Operator's Manual would give the basic information required for introduction to precision autorotation. The normally acceptable autorotation airspeed ranges for the various models of helicopters for aviators having average skills vary from slightly less than slow cruise values to slightly higher than cruise values (ranges 2 through 5 of figures 2-91 and 2-92). In airspeeds of range 2 to midpoint range 3 of figure 2-92 note that a slight change of airspeed results in a large selection in rates of descent; therefore, this is the best precision airspeed glide slope. An aviator in a steady state autorotation in this airspeed range may advance or retreat the point of ground contact noticeably by increasing or decreasing the airspeed by as little as 5 knots. Airspeeds of less than range 2 yield increasingly high rates of descent.

Figure 2-92 shows eight example entry points for the entire forced landing and precision autorotation envelope. These entry points show positions on the front side, back side, and inside of the precision glide slope. Before considering each of these entry points in detail, some important general considerations to be remembered are as follows:

□ The best precision airspeed range as shown in figure 2-91 is between range 2 and range 3. When plotted in profile, this airspeed spread becomes the precision glide slope or the cone of precision.

□ The main effort in performing the precision autorotation at entry points 1, 2, 4, 5, and 6, is to intercept and stay inside the precision glide slope. The precision glide slope must be intercepted as soon as possible; then a steady state airspeed is established and tested, holding a slow cruise attitude.

□ The circle of action point (fig 2-92) is the circle of action or the point of collision (which is two or three helicopter lengths short of the touchdown), where (to the eye) the helicopter would hit the ground if collective pitch were not applied.

□ For recognition purposes, entry point 6 can be considered as the entry position for the familiar standard autorotation.

□ The precision autorotation flight envelope ends at 100 feet. A basic type termination can be made thereafter to a touchdown point (fig 2-92), provided the airspeed is within allowable tolerance of range 3 and the rate of descent is normal. See other terminations in figure 2-93.

□ For maneuver repeatability, exact attitudes must be used or noted throughout the autorotation. The center of attention is split between attitude and the circle of action point. All other references such as airspeed, rotor RPM, etc., are read in a running cross-check.

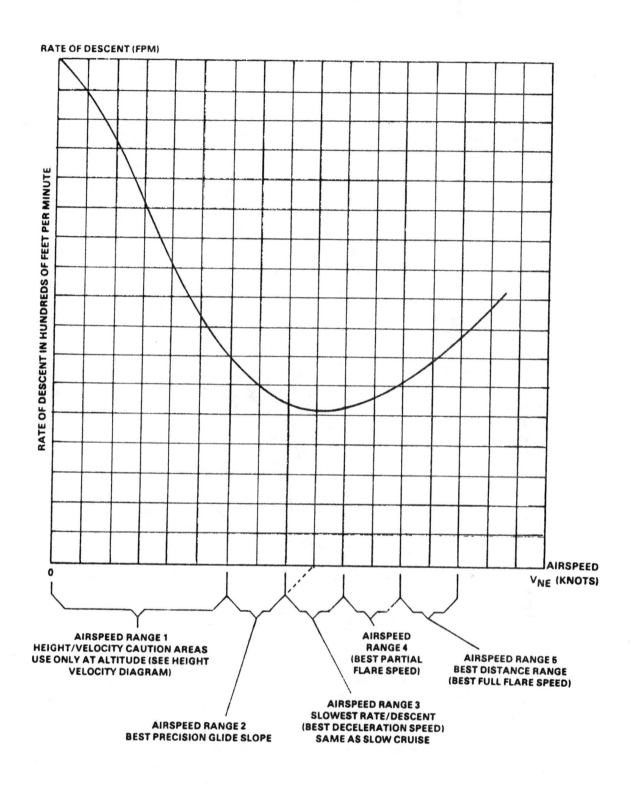

FIGURE 2-91. STEADY STATE AUTOROTATION RATE OF DESCENT (FPM) FOR VARIOUS AIRSPEEDS.

THIS PAGE
INTENTIONALLY LEFT BLANK

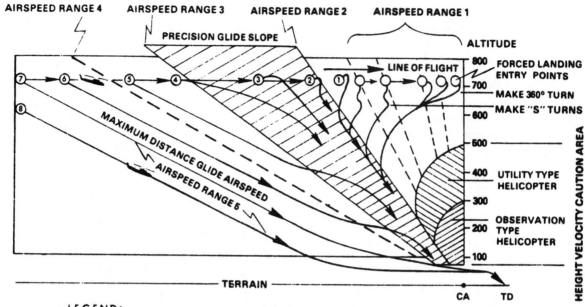

FIGURE 2-92. FORCE LANDING AUTOROTATION FLIGHT ENVELOPE FOR TYPICAL HELICOPTERS.

☐ The airspeed values and restrictions of the height velocity diagram must be scaled up to comply with the performance charts of larger helicopters. Height velocity diagrams are based on a standard day at sea level, and the envelopes must be expanded in proportion to increasing density altitude (fig 2-94).

Procedures described under Entry Points No. 1, 2, and 3 that follow are for discussion only and should not be performed in training. Considerable risk is involved in performing these maneuvers. They are included so the pilot will have the knowledge and can attempt these type landings if required during an actual forward landing.

☐ *Entry Point No. 1:* (Not a training maneuver.)

● In the area of entry point No. 1 (fig 2-92), the touchdown point appears to be almost vertical to the pilot.

● At cruise airspeed into the wind and at 700 feet above ground level (AGL) when the throttle is reduced, lower collective pitch, hold heading, and decelerate promptly for speed reduction climb—stopping all apparent groundspeed at the intended landing spot.

● Hold the nose high attitude until the airspeed goes through 15 knots, then slowly lower the attitude at a rate so as to establish a 0-knot reading and a slow cruise or hovering attitude. (Optional, make "S" turns holding range 2 airspeed.)

● Settle vertically; a headwind will cause a slight rearward movement.

● When it appears that the helicopter is about to intercept the precision glide slope, lower attitude smoothly and progressively to a point slightly below the normal takeoff acceleration attitude.

● *When the airspeed reaches between range 2 and range 3, rotate to a slow cruise attitude.

● Watch the circle of action point for evidence of overshooting or undershooting.

● If undershooting, lower attitude to gain 5 knots; then return attitude to slow cruise (for further reading of the circle of action point).

● *If overshooting, raise attitude to lose 5 knots; then return attitude to slow cruise (for further reading of the circle of action point).

● At 100 feet, if airspeed is within allowable tolerance of range 3, terminate as in a standard autorotation for a landing at the touchdown point.

● At 100 feet, if airspeed is range 2, hold slow cruise attitude to approximately 50 feet; then rotate to the normal deceleration attitude.

*In reading the precision line of descent, observation of the circle of action point is reliable only when the attitude is at slow cruise and when a steady state autorotation is in progress (no deceleration, no acceleration).

● Touchdown on TD point as in basic autorotation touchdown.

□ *Entry Point No. 2:* (Not a training maneuver.)

● In the area of entry point No. 2 (fig 2-92), the student estimates that he is almost beyond the precision glide slope.

● At cruise airspeed and at 700 feet AGL, when the throttle is reduced, lower collective pitch, hold heading, and decelerate promptly for a speed reduction climb— stopping all apparent groundspeed at the intended landing spot.

● As the apparent groundspeed reaches 0 knots, lower attitude to the slow cruise attitude. (The airspeed will now be equal to, or near, the wind velocity.)

● Settle vertically and continue as indicated in exercise "Entry Point No. 1" to remain within the precision glide slope.

□ *Entry Point No. 3:* (Not a training maneuver.)

● In the area of entry point No. 3 (fig 2-92), the student estimates that he is well into the precision glide slope.

● At cruise airspeed and at 700 feet AGL, when the throttle is reduced, lower collective pitch, hold heading, and make speed reduction climb.

● As the airspeed approaches between range 2 and range 3 (depending upon the headwind effect on groundspeed), lower attitude to the slow cruise attitude for a steady state autorotation. Then proceed as indicated in exercise "Entry Point No. 1" to remain within the precision glide slope.

☐ *Entry Point No. 4:*

● In the area of entry point No. 4 (fig 2-92), the student estimates that he is just short of the precision glide slope.

● At cruise airspeed and at 700 feet AGL, when the throttle is reduced, lower collective pitch, hold heading, and decelerate smoothly. This will cause a lifting up to the precision glide slope.

● As the airspeed approaches between range 2 and range 3 (depending upon the headwind effect on groundspeed), lower attitude to the slow cruise attitude for a steady state autorotation. Then proceed as indicated in exercise "Entry Point No. 1," to remain within the precision glide slope.

Note: Exercise No. 4 is the example to use when demonstrating an ideal precision autorotation.

☐ *Entry Point No. 5:*

● In the area of entry point No. 5 (fig 2-92), the student estimates that he is well short of the precision glide slope.

● At cruise airspeed and at 700 feet when the throttle is reduced, lower collective pitch, hold heading, cruise attitude, and rotor RPM for best distance. (Hold crab, rather than slip, for best distance.)

● When it appears that the precision glide slope is just ahead, do a partial deceleration. This will cause lifting up to the precision glide slope.

● As airspeed approaches between range 2 and range 3, rotate attitude to slow cruise for a steady state autorotation and proceed as indicated in exercise "Entry Point No. 1," to remain within the precision glide slope.

☐ *Entry Point No. 6:*

● In the area of entry point No. 6 (fig 2-92), the student estimates that he is almost too far back for interception of the precision glide slope.

● He proceeds as in entry point No. 5 with possible interception of the precision glide slope further down the line of descent. However, he may decide to proceed as for entry point No. 7.

☐ *Entry Point No. 7:*

● In the area of entry point No. 7 (fig 2-92), the student estimates that he cannot intercept the precision glide slope.

● At cruise airspeed and at 700 feet AGL when the throttle is cut, lower collective pitch, and hold heading and cruise attitude for best distance.

● The line of descent appears to be a spot well short of the touchdown point.

● At approximately 200 feet, begin a smooth lifting partial deceleration, converting speed to lift. This will change the line of descent toward the touchdown point.

● By regulating the rate and amount of deceleration from 200 feet on, a basic type termination can be made at the touchdown point.

□ *Entry Point No. 8:*

● This exercise is identical to the exercise for entry point No. 7 except that the entry is set up farther away from the precision glide slope than it was at No. 7.

● The line of descent appears to be to a point 100 feet (or more) short of the normal circle of action point.

● Hold best distance attitude, rotor RPM, and pedal trim. Upon reaching 40 to 60 feet altitude, execute a full deceleration which is regulated in rate and amount of attitude rotation, so as to arrive at the touchdown point at the end of the deceleration.

● Allow the helicopter to settle to 15 to 20 feet; apply initial collective pitch; rotate attitude to level landing attitude; and apply a firm positive collective pitch in the amount and at a rate necessary to cushion the landing.

THAT LAST 100 FEET

For purposes of clarity, assume that the autorotation ends at 100 feet and that the power-off landing procedure begins there. The accepted method of executing a power-off landing for rotary-wing aircraft is to obtain a smooth tradeoff of airspeed for lift during the last 100 feet. Ideally, beginning at 100 feet, airspeed is converted to additional lift by deceleration. The deceleration is so timed and applied that the rate of descent and the forward speed are reduced just before touchdown to the slowest rates possible for the existing conditions.

□ *Potential energy available for power-off landing.* At 100 feet, the pilot must begin spending stored flight energies; i.e., the forward velocity of the helicopter and, just before touchdown, the rotational energy of the main rotor. At 100 feet, he can predict with accuracy the amount of potential energy (deceleration or cyclic lifting power) available for the power-off landing. He can also predict the effectiveness of applying collective pitch to cushion the touchdown.

□ *Reducing the rate of descent and slowing the groundspeed.* All the heavy aerodynamic work of reducing the rate of descent and slowing the groundspeed should be a result of the pilot's effecting some form of deceleration, down to approximately 15 feet. Thereafter, his use of collective pitch further slows (at times, delays) the descent and then cushions the touchdown. See figure 2-93 for predictable conditions for the power-off landing.

□ *Terms and definitions.* The following terms and definitions should be understood for the discussion of power-off landings in succeeding paragraphs.

● *Attitude Rotation*—A preplanned or scheduled change of aircraft attitude at some specific point in a maneuver sequence.

● *Deceleration*—A tradeoff of airspeed for lift while holding or maintaining a relatively continuous line of descent.

● *Partial Deceleration*—A tradeoff of airspeed for lift which results in a moderate change to the line of flight.

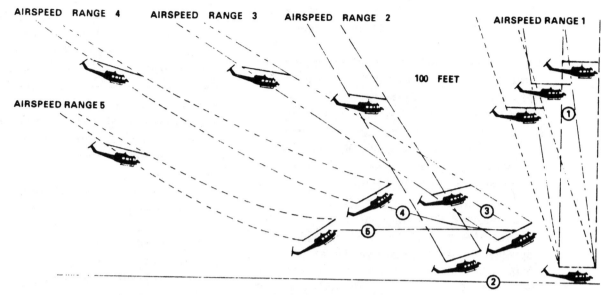

FIGURE 2-93. THAT LAST 100 FEET.

• *Full Deceleration*—A tradeoff of airspeed for lift which results in a substantial change to the line of flight. In autorotation at the appropriate altitude, the descending line of flight is changed by converting airspeed to lift, so as to parallel the ground for some distance.

NOTE: The terms deceleration, partial deceleration, and full deceleration do not apply to the attitude rotation per se, but to the change in lift and/or the change in the line of flight which results from the attitude rotation.

☐ *Conditions.* Figure 2-93 shows the airspeed conditions at 100 feet and the following paragraphs describe the landing sequences resulting from those airspeed conditions.

• *Condition 5 (airspeed range 5, fig 2-93).* Condition 5 exists at 100 feet with airspeed range 5 (best distance-gliding airspeed, see appropriate aircraft Operator's Manual). In condition 5, the helicopter is descending on a very narrow rotor profile to the line of descent. The helicopter is then encountering a large volume of air per second. This can produce exceptional lifting forces when the attitude is rotated smoothly and progressively and the full rotor diameter profile is presented to (or against) the line of descending flight. This attitude rotation is usually accomplished at 30 to 60 feet, depending on the aircraft.

The added lift generated by the full deceleration is so great that the descent will be stopped and the line of flight will parallel the ground for some distance. As the deceleration ends, with the density-altitude, wind, or gross weight favorable, the helicopter settles gently to a point where the pilot applies initial pitch. This is followed by the pilot's final application of collective pitch for a soft touchdown and a near zero ground run. All of this is predictable at 100 feet.

2-81

● *Condition 4 (airspeed range 4, fig 2-93).* Condition 4 exists at 100 feet, with airspeed range 4, in which the helicopter is descending on a narrow rotor profile to the line of descent. A smooth and progressive attitude change (deceleration) which presents a full rotor diameter profile to (or against) the line of descent will alter the line of descent and add lift. When properly timed, this added lift will greatly reduce the rate of descent and forward speed prior to the initial collective pitch application. The deceleration may also be used to increase rotor RPM prior to collective pitch application. All of this is predictable at 100 feet.

NOTE: The full or partial deceleration termination is necessary for a zero ground run. The full or partial deceleration is mandatory for helicopters having low rotor inertia with light unweighted blades and/or poor collective pitch effectiveness at termination.

● *Condition 3 (airspeed range 3, fig 2-93).* Condition 3 exists at 100 feet, with airspeed range 3, in which the helicopter is descending on slightly less than a full rotor diameter profile to the line of descent; translational lift is near maximum effect and the rate of descent is minimum. The pilot should know that a smooth and progressive rotation of attitude which presents a full rotor diameter profile to (or against) the line of descent will result in an effective deceleration.

This deceleration, while not noticeably changing the line of descent, will reduce the rate of descent and the forward speed to a point where collective pitch energy will be quite effective. When the deceleration is timed correctly, the descent is often stopped completely when initial pitch is applied by the pilot. This still leaves adequate pitch to delay and then cushion the touchdown (when wind, density, altitude, or weight are favorable) resulting in a relatively short ground run. All of this is predictable at 100 feet.

● *Condition 2 (airspeed range 2, fig 2-93).* Condition 2 exists at 100 feet, with airspeed range 2, when the helicopter is descending on nearly a full rotor diameter profile. The pilot knows or should know that nothing will be gained by an attitude rotation; that he should hold a steady attitude to maintain the speed, at least down to 50 feet; and that, of the five conditions, condition 2 will give the longest ground run. Therefore, at about 50 feet, he should begin a progressive attitude change until a slight rearward tilt of the rotor occurs just prior to his application of collective pitch. The attitude change will not supply additional lift, but it will add a rearward component of lift during his pitch application. This will help slow and shorten the ground run.

It is predictable that, having no effective deceleration lift in progress (during the last 100 feet), the application of collective pitch alone will not provide sufficient lifting and braking action to have appreciable effect in delaying the touchdown and slowing the ground run. The ground run will be approximately three to four lengths. All of this is predictable at 100 feet.

The hidden danger in condition 2 lies in the frequency of occurrence of this condition. Another consideration is that condition 2 falls on the borderline of the height/velocity diagram. Often a wind gradient and/or high density altitude condition can then cause an increase in the rate of descent, thus increasing the lift demands on the collective pitch application. The resulting accident summary usually states that the damage was caused by a late and insufficient application of collective pitch. Actually, the error occurred earlier — at 100 feet. It was due to a lack of knowledge, cross-check, projection, and prediction. When condition 2 is performed knowledgeably, with normal atmospheric and gross weights, it is considered a SAFE operation.

● *Condition 1 (airspeed range 1, fig 2-93).* Condition 1 falls in the restricted areas of the height/velocity diagram. It exists at 100 feet, with airspeed range 1, when the helicopter is descending on a full rotor diameter profile to the line of descent. There is a high sink rate; no deceleration lift is possible. Due to a wind gradient, gusts, or wind shift, this condition may suddenly occur in the last 100 feet of descent. The entire rate of descent must then be stopped by the application of collective pitch alone. Usually the lift produced is insufficient for safe landings. Condition 1 may also cause obvious or hidden damage to the helicopter due to hard landings. Such damage might be acceptable for an actual engine failure, but it is never acceptable for normal training practice and a termination with power is necessary. All of this is predictable at 100 feet.

HEIGHT/VELOCITY DIAGRAM

A typical height/velocity diagram or "dead man's curve" is shown in A, figure 2-94. The caution areas carry the warning "Avoid continuous operations—engine failure while operating within these caution areas is likely to result in damage to the helicopter."

Caution area (A) of diagram A in figure 2-94 is computed from engineering data, with the following factors included:

☐ Rate of descent required to drive the rotor in autorotation, for each 10-knot increment of airspeed (from 0 through red line or top speed) for the specific helicopter configuration. See diagram B, figure 2-94.

☐ Rotor inertia characteristics or the rotor RPM decay rate, from the moment of engine failure or until engine failure cues become available to the pilot. The pilot reaction time must be added after the cues become available. It is also based on the rotor RPM decay rate experienced while sufficient vertical descent is achieved to drive the rotor.

☐ Translational lift values and sink rates for each height/velocity condition, with the resulting rotor RPM and "pitch pull" energy then available for cushioning ground impact.

☐ Designed stress limitations of the landing gear and "hard landing" damage-risk to other components.

The combinations of altitude and airspeed which define the avoid areas of the height/velocity diagram are peculiar to each type of helicopter. They are dependent upon gross weight, pressure altitude, ambient temperature, velocity, engine power available, number of engines operating, and rotor speed. Typically, data in the aircraft's flight manual is presented graphically for sea level, standard temperature conditions at design gross weight. Scaling factors for other conditions may be noted in the text and should be observed.

The diagrams are plotted for a "steady state" constant airspeed and constant altitude; therefore, they do not apply to climbing flight. Engine failure occurring while climbing through any of the height/velocity combinations will usually result in damage to the helicopter. During a climb, the helicopter is operating at higher power settings and blade angles of attack. An engine failure will cause rapid rotor RPM decay because the helicopter must stop going upward, then begin and reach its descent in order to drive the rotor, stabilize the RPM; then increase the RPM to its normal range. The rate of descent must reach a value that is normal for the airspeed at the moment. Since altitude is insufficient for this sequence, the pilot ends up with the helicopter having decaying RPM, increasing sink rate, no deceleration lift, little translational lift, and little response to his application of collective pitch to cushion ground impact.

Operations in the caution area (A) of diagram A, figure 2-94, are much less dangerous during descending flight through any included height/velocity

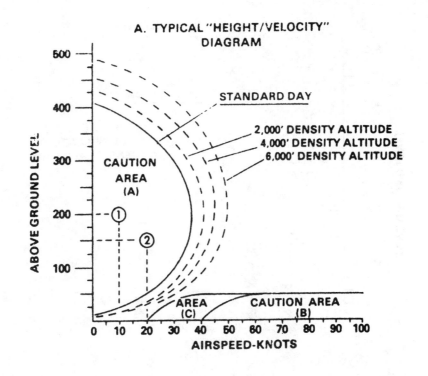

A. TYPICAL "HEIGHT/VELOCITY" DIAGRAM

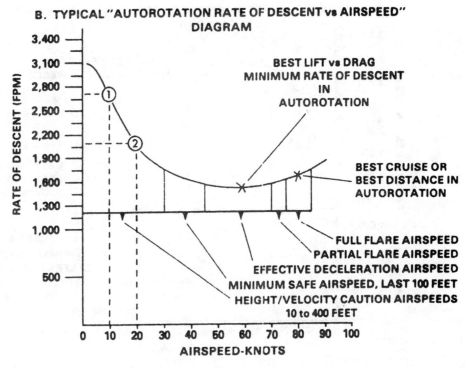

B. TYPICAL "AUTOROTATION RATE OF DESCENT vs AIRSPEED" DIAGRAM

FIGURE 2-94. HEIGHT/VELOCITY DIAGRAM.

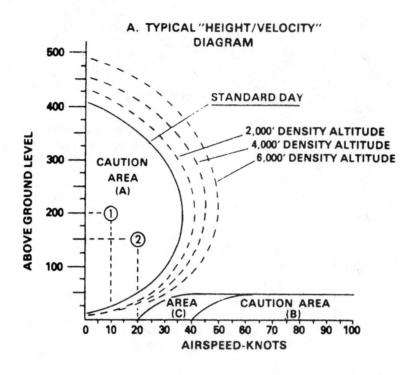

A. TYPICAL "HEIGHT/VELOCITY" DIAGRAM

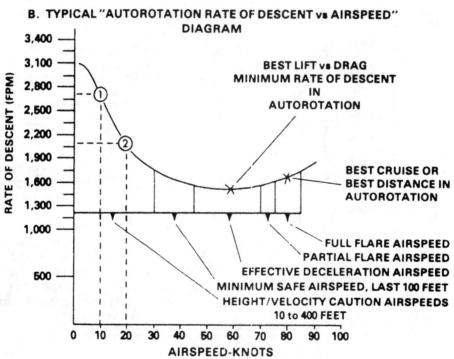

B. TYPICAL "AUTOROTATION RATE OF DESCENT vs AIRSPEED" DIAGRAM

FIGURE 2-94. HEIGHT/VELOCITY DIAGRAM.

combination, provided a landing site is available.

Caution area (B) of diagram A, figure 2-94, warns against continuous operations in certain low altitude/airspeed/terrain combinations. These restrictions are based upon:

1 Pilot recognition time of engine failure cues.

2 Time required to rotate from nose-low forward mode to a slight or moderate nose-high attitude.

3 Altitude loss during **1** and **2** above, and groundspeed remaining as tail wheel/skid/guard/cone hits the ground or other obstacles.

NOTE: The similarity between **1** , **2** , and **3** above and the usual "low-level autorotation," as practiced to a runway, is almost nonexistent. The solution is for pilots to completely avoid operations in area "B" unless dictated by the tactical mission.

Area (C) of diagram A, figure 2-94, can be used over open level terrain or runways where obstacle evasion or direction change is not required and a short ground run is possible. This condition is similar to the usual practice low-level autorotation.

At slow airspeeds with an available landing site (as a general rule), the aviator should allow 300 feet for small helicopters and 500 to 600 feet for larger helicopters to set up a steady state autorotation and complete a resonably safe landing.

An engine failure (A, fig 2-94) at 10 knots, 200 feet, requires 2,700 fpm rate of descent (B, fig 2-94) to drive the rotor at normal RPM.

An engine failure at 20 knots (A, fig 2-94), 150 feet, requires 2,100 fpm rate of descent (B, fig 2-94) to drive the rotor at normal RPM.

The rates of descent in examples (1) and (2) of diagram B, figure 2-94, will not be attained; therefore, rotor RPM will decay. No deceleration lift is possible to slow the rate of descent, and rotor inertia (RPM) will be low for the collective pitch application and touchdown. These combined effects will increase the possibility of a hard landing and structural damage to the helicopter.

REMEMBER

Helicopter pilots are often asked to accomplish a wide variety of tasks. They should not operate in the caution areas of the height/velocity diagram unless the specific mission requires it. Certain flight operations require pilots to operate within the caution area of the H/V diagram. Consequently, pilots should have a thorough knowledge of the specific aircrafts H/V diagram and pertinent emergency procedures.

CHAPTER 3

COMMON
HELICOPTER
FLIGHT TECHNIQUES

KNOWLEDGE, PLANNING AND PREDICTION

Basic flying techniques described in this chapter are generally applicable to all aircraft. The attitude flying concept introduced and enlarged during primary flight training promotes learning and establishes sound habit patterns. It provides for easy transition into larger, more complex aircraft and promotes smooth progression through instrument flight training and into operational status in an aviation unit. The mechanics and techniques of flight, correctly learned in early training, produce aviators who are highly standardized. New aviators should be encouraged to study and use the basic concepts of attitude contact flying and later attitude instrument flying. They should be encouraged to develop a working knowledge of how the aircraft components and vital systems function. With these knowledges and skills, pilots can adjust their flight performance to the requirements of future flight assignments.

Pilot performance is built upon adequate knowledge, thorough *planning*, and the ability to project or *predict* what the aircraft will do. Coordination, feel, and control touch are also important factors, but they are secondary to the first three. Subject matter for aviation training, according to these principles, is listed below. Emphasis should be on the subject areas in the order listed.

CONTENTS

☐ Knowledge of aerodynamics, physics, and mechanics of flight.

☐ Specific knowledge of the systems, components, controls, and structures of the helicopter being used.

☐ Knowledge of the methods and rules of *attitude flying* which are similar to the rules of attitude instrument flying in FM 1-5.

☐ Specific knowledge of the breakdown of attitudes and cross-checks for each maneuver; and development in dividing attention and cross-checking outward from a specific center of attention for each segment of a maneuver.

☐ Development of smooth and coordinated physical application of control; and the ability to hold attitudes and power settings or to change attitude and power as necessary to perform a maneuver.

Physical application of the controls is probably less important in the initial stages of training than the other four subject areas listed above. Physical skill is developed most rapidly after the aviator has mastered the first four subject areas. Aviators must learn *what to do* before they can develop the physical skills to perform a maneuver.

ATTITUDE FLYING

Aircraft attitude is the position of the aircraft in relation to the horizon. Attitude is controlled about three imaginary axes: the *longitudinal* axis, the *lateral* axis, and the *vertical* axis (fig 3-1). When an aircraft banks (or rolls), it changes attitude about the longitudinal axis. Attitude change about the lateral axis is called *pitch*, and refers to raising or lowering the aircraft nose in relation to the horizon. Yaw (turning right or left) is attitude change about the vertical axis. During flight it is possible for an aircraft to change attitude about only one of these axes at a time. Frequently, however, attitude change will include movement about all three axes simultaneously.

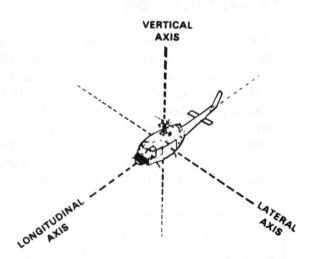

FIGURE 3-1. AXES ABOUT WHICH AIRCRAFT ATTITUDE IS CONTROLLED.

The attitude of the aircraft in relation to the horizon and the power applied are the only two elements of control in all aircraft. Proper use of these two elements of control will produce any desired maneuver within the capability of the aircraft. Therefore, all maneuvers *must* be based solidly upon attitude and power control references.

Aircraft attitude and power are modified by the pilot in two ways; one, the time of application of an attitude or power change, and two, the rate of change of an attitude or power adjustment.

Keeping the basic control elements and modifiers in mind, the pilot cross-checks for a running awareness of what the aircraft is doing at the moment. Using knowledge gained from experience, the pilot can project what the aircraft is going to do based on the power setting and attitude that is being maintained. Attitude and power changes are smoothly applied to cause the aircraft to perform the desired maneuver. The result is attitude flying.

ATTUTUDE CONTROL AND AIRSPEED

Airspeed is controlled by adjusting pitch attitude about the lateral axis of the aircraft. To hold a desired airspeed, or make properly controlled changes of airspeed, the pilot must learn the aircraft pitch attitudes that will result in acceleration, deceleration, hover, and the desired cruising airspeeds.

For a given power setting, there is a pitch attitude and airspeed that will maintain altitude. If power is constant, an increase in airspeed (resulting from a change of pitch attitude) will cause loss of altitude. Conversely, a reduction of airspeed with power constant will usually cause a gain of altitude.

If power is increased while pitch attitude is held constant, a constant airspeed and climb will result. If the power setting is decreased while pitch attitude is held constant, airspeed will remain constant and a descent will result.

ATTUTUDE CONTROL AND COORDINATED TURNS

During coordinated flight, turns are a result of bank attitude control about the longitudinal axis of the aircraft. To hold a desired heading, the pilot must keep the rotor disk laterally level in relation to the horizon.

Turns are accomplished by banking (rolling) the aircraft about the longitudinal axis until the rotor disk is tilted laterally. Rate of turn is controlled by the degree the rotor disk is tilted. Aviators must learn to smoothly bank the aircraft to a degree of lateral tilt that will produce the desired rate of turn.

Stopping a turn is accomplished by smoothly rolling the aircraft level. Rollout is started before the desired heading is reached, so the turn is stopped on the desired heading.

Turning flight is accomplished by changing part of the vertical lifting force (A, fig 3-2) toward the horizontal. The turn produces centrifugal force which tends to move the aircraft toward the outside of the turn (B, fig 3-2). The resultant of weight and centrifugal force is outward and downward and is greater than the weight of the aircraft in A, figure 3-2. The resultant of weight and centrifugal force must be overcome by an addition of total lift or the aircraft will lose altitude during a turn. Aircraft C, figure 3-2, shows an increase of total lift as a result of increased collective pitch and power. Total lift now equals the total of centrifugal force and weight, so the aircraft will turn without losing altitude.

The resultant of weight and centrifugal force during turns produces an increased load factor on the aircraft. Load factor is the total load imposed on an aircraft, divided by the weight of the aircraft, and is expressed in G units. Load factor during a turn varies with the angle of bank (fig 3-3). Airspeed during a turn does not affect load factor, because for a given bank angle the rate of turn decreases with increased airspeed, resulting in no change of centrifugal force. Note that for a 60-degree bank, the load factor for any aircraft is 2 Gs regardless of airspeed (fig 3-3). This means that a 10,000-pound aircraft in a 60-degree bank will, in effect, exert 20,000 pounds of force on the aircraft structure. Bank angles

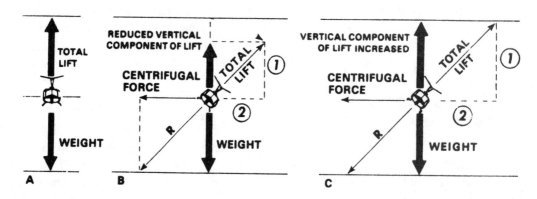

① = VERTICAL COMPONENT OF LIFT
② = HORIZONTAL COMPONENT OF LIFT

Lift and weight are equal on aircraft A.

A and B have the same collective pitch and power setting, therefore, because weight and centrifugal force are acting together and increasing the load factor, vertical lift on B is less than weight.

Aircraft C has increased collective pitch and power to make vertical lift equal weight.

FIGURE 3-2. LOSS OF VERTICAL LIFT DURING TURNS.

up to 30° produce only moderate increases in *load factor* which are acceptable under most flight conditions. The load factor rises at an increasing rate for banks over 30° (fig 3-3), and may produce unacceptable disk loading depending upon the aircraft gross weight and flight conditions.

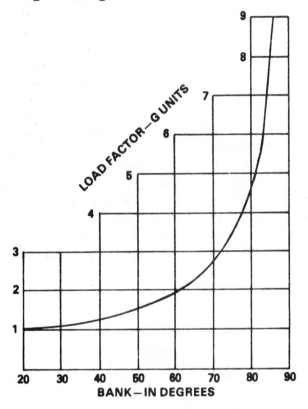

FIGURE 3-3. LOAD FACTORS IN VARIOUS ANGLES OF BANK DURING LEVEL TURNS.

POWER CONTROL AND RESULTING ALTITUDE, CLIMB, OR DESCENT

Altitude is a result of power control. To hold a desired altitude or make changes of altitude, the aviator must apply the power settings that will produce the desired climb or descent when combined with the possible combinations of attitude and airspeed. Power settings that are normal for hover, climb, cruise, slow cruise, and descent must be used if precise control of altitude is desired. The pilot must also be able to adjust power to compensate for variation in atmospheric conditions and aircraft gross weight.

For a given attitude and airspeed, there is a power setting that will maintain altitude. If a climb is desired with a constant attitude and airspeed, power must be increased above that required to maintain altitude. If a descent is desired with constant attitude and airspeed, power must be reduced below the power required for maintaining altitude.

A constant altitude is maintained by minor pitch attitude adjustments and by power adjustments as necessary. After the altitude is stabilized and the desired airspeed is established, any deviation from altitude will result in an airspeed change as long as the altitude is changing. When the altitude is again stabilized, the airspeed will return to its previous indication provided the power is maintained at the previous setting. If airspeed is high due to loss of altitude, the excess airspeed may be used to return the aircraft to the desired altitude and airspeed by an upward pitch attitude adjustment. Conversely, with a gain in altitude and an accompanying loss of airspeed, the excess altitude may be utilized by a downward pitch attitude adjustment to return the aircraft to the desired airspeed and altitude.

HEADING CONTROL AND THE ANTITORQUE PEDALS

The primary purpose of the antitorque pedals is to counteract torque. However, the antitorque system usually is designed to have surplus thrust, far beyond that required to counteract torque. This additional thrust, designed into the tail rotor system, is used to provide positive and negative thrust for taxi direction control and to counteract the crosswind effect on the fuselage during hovering operations. In certain helicopter configurations, care must be exercised in using the thrust power of the antitorque system, since damage to the tail pylon area can result from overstress during fast rate hovering pedal turns and during taxi conditions over rough ground.

There are three separate modes of control for correct pedal use. Each of these modes should be analyzed and treated separately by the aviator.

☐ The *first* group includes normal helicopter operations below 50 feet, during which the fuselage is alined with a distant point. This group includes taking off to and landing from a hover, the stationary hover, the moving hover, the takeoff and climb slip control, and the approach slip control.

☐ The *second* group includes coordinated flight and all operations above 50 feet which require pedal use to aline and hold the fuselage into the relative wind.

☐ The *third* group includes proper pedal use in turns. Coordinated turns (at altitude) require the proper use of pedals to keep the fuselage into the relative wind as the bank is initiated, established, and maintained.

Heading and track control for operations below 50 feet.

☐ Taking off to and landing from a hover require that pedals be repositioned to hold and maintain the nose alinement with a distant reference point. The aviator uses an imaginary line to a distant object and applies pedal to position and maintain the line of sight from his seat through the cyclic and gap between his pedals (fig 3-4).

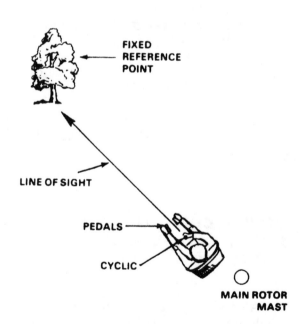

FIXED REFERENCE POINT

LINE OF SIGHT

PEDALS

CYCLIC

MAIN ROTOR MAST

FIGURE 3-4. HEADING ALINEMENT DURING HOVERING.

Aviators in either seat use the same distant reference point with no appreciable error. Fuselage alinement to hovering or takeoff direction is shown in figure 3-5.

☐ During the moving hover and the initial climb to 50 feet, pedals control heading as in figure 3-5; and cyclic control is used for direction and lateral positioning over the intended track as in figure 3-6. Using peripheral vision (and cross-check), the helicopter should be positioned with lateral cyclic so the imaginary line is seen running through position 1 (fig 3-6) during taxi or run on landings, and position 2 for hovering and climb through 20 feet. The line should be seen between pedals as shown at position 3 for all altitudes over 20 feet, with all track reference points lined up and passing between pedals in passage over each point.

☐ In crosswind operations, the combined use of pedals and cyclic as described above results in a side slip, commonly referred to as a slip. The aviator does not consciously think "slip," for he is automatically in a true slip if he holds the fuselage alined on a distant object with pedals (fig 3-4) and maintains positioning over the line with cyclic (fig 3-6).

FUSELAGE ALINEMENT TO HOVERING OR TAKEOFF DIRECTION

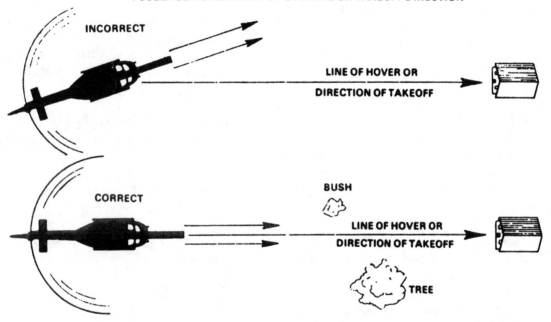

FIGURE 3-5. USE OF REFERENCES FOR HEADING CONTROL BELOW 50 FEET.

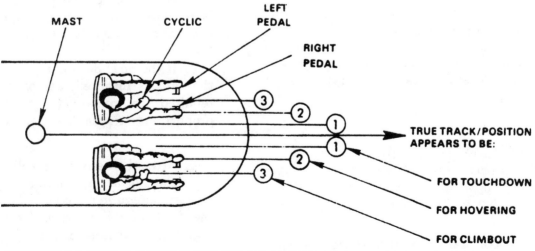

FIGURE 3-6. LATERAL POSITIONING REQUIRED TO MAINTAIN DESIRED GROUND TRACK.

Heading and track control for operations above 50 feet.

☐ For coordinated flight above 50 feet, the pedals assume a purely antitorque role and are promptly repositioned to a climb pedal setting upon reaching 50 feet. This pedal action alines the fuselage with the relative wind, rather than with a distant object.

● The helicopter is now in coordinated flight, during which the cyclic controls fuselage heading; the rotor disk is level laterally; and the ball is centered.

● The track is now controlled by a coordinated cyclic bank and turn to a heading that will result in the desired track. Tracking toward and over selected ground reference points will cause these reference points to pass directly under the aviator's seat cushion.

☐ Power changes require sufficient coordinated pedal to prevent the fuselage from yawing left or right. When the power change is completed, cross-check the new pedal setting and lateral trim of the fuselage.

☐ Generally, the average single rotor helicopter will have pedal settings which are normal for various power/speed combinations. Coordinate these settings with power changes and hold in cross-check (for all operations and coordinated flight above 50 feet).

☐ Rigging of pedal control linkage will vary in helicopters of the same type. Therefore, in steady climb, cruise, descent, or autorotation, with pedals set, cross-check:

● Turn-and-slip indicator for a centered ball. Pedal into the low ball and note the exact pedal setting required when ball is centered.

● Door frames or windshield frames for lateral level trim. Pedal into the low side and note the exact pedal setting required.

● Main rotor tip-path plane. It should be the same distance above the horizon on each side. For level rotor, pedal into the low side.

☐ In semirigid main rotor configurations, note the lateral hang of the fuselage at a hover (into the wind). If the fuselage is not level, due to a lateral CG displacement, then the one-side low condition must be accepted as level; thereafter, in flight (air work over 50 feet) adjust pedals for a lateral trim of one-side low as existed at a hover. Even though the fuselage is one-side low, the rotor is laterally level to the horizon, and the helicopter is in trimmed flight.

Pedal use in turns. Use of pedal to enter and maintain a turn requires study and experiment for the particular helicopter being flown.

☐ To determine if pedal is required for a coordinated entry to bank and turn—

● Start at cruise airspeed with the correct pedal setting for lateral trim in straight-and-level flight.

● Begin a bank with cyclic only. Use no pedal.

● Note whether the nose turns in proportion to the bank.

☐ If the nose begins to turn as the bank is initiated, no pedal is required for the entry to a turn in this helicopter.

☐ If the nose does not begin to turn as the bank is initiated, use only that pedal required to make the nose turn in proportion to the bank and entry.

☐ After the bank is established, anticipate the normal requirement in all helicopters to require a slight pedal pressure in the direction of the turn for coordinated flight and a centered ball.

A traffic pattern is useful to control the flow of traffic, particularly at nonradio-controlled airports or landing areas. It affords a measure of safety, separation, protection, and administrative control over arriving, departing, and circling aircraft. During nontactical training, a precise traffic pattern is flown to promote knowledge, planning, prediction, and flight discipline. All pattern procedures must be strictly followed so that every aviator working in the circuit and transient aviators arriving and departing, can determine at a glance the intentions of the other aviators.

When approaching a radio-controlled airport in a helicopter, it is possible to expedite traffic by stating, for example:

☐ (Call sign or aircraft serial number) Army helicopter 16123.

☐ (Position) 10 miles east.

☐ (Request) for landing and hover to. . .

The tower will often clear you direct to an approach point or to a particular runway intersection nearest your destination point. At uncontrolled airports, adhere strictly to standard practices and patterns.

Figure 3-7 depicts a typical nontactical traffic pattern with general procedures outlined. If there is no identifiable helicopter traffic pattern, set up one inside the normal airplane pattern. Use touchdown and takeoff points to one side of the active runway. If you intend to land on the runway, approach to the near end; then hover clear of the runway immediately.

To fly a good traffic pattern, visualize a rectangular ground track and—

☐ Follow good outbound tracking on takeoff and climbout, with steady climb airspeed.

☐ Turn usually less than 90° for drift correction on the turn to crosswind leg, so as to track 90° to the takeoff leg.

☐ Select a point on the horizon for turn to downwind leg, so as to fly a track parallel to the takeoff and landing direction. Maintain a constant airspeed and altitude.

☐ Turn usually more than 90° for drift correction on the turn to base leg. Change attitude to slow cruise to establish approach entry airspeed. Change power and pedals to descend at approximately 500 feet per minute, or to lose 5 miles per hour for each 100 feet of descent. Watch far reference point for turn to final approach leg (fig 3-8).

☐ Turn short or beyond 90° on the turn to final, depending upon the crosswind condition. Before entering approach (or not later than the last 50 feet of the approach), establish a slip with fuselage on line with the line of approach and the helicopter positioned over the line of approach.

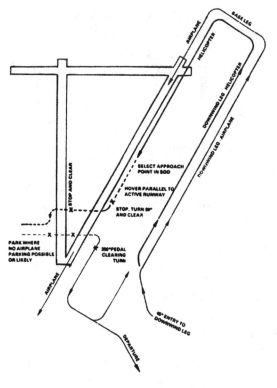

FIGURE 3-7. TYPICAL TRAFFIC PATTERN

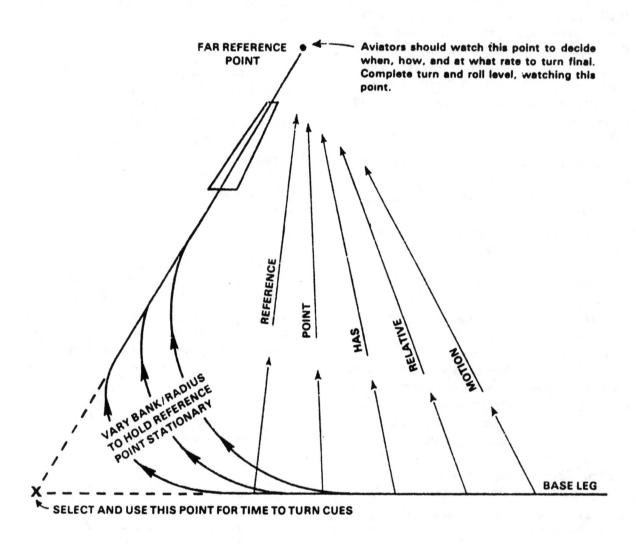

FIGURE 3-8. TURN TO FINAL APPROACH.

CHAPTER 4

NORMAL

FIELD OPERATIONS

BASIC CONSIDERATIONS

For the purpose of this discussion, a *confined area* is any area where the flight of the helicopter is limited in some direction by terrain or the presence of obstructions, natural or manmade. For example, a clearing in the woods, the top of a mountain, the slope of a hill, or the deck of a ship can each be regarded as a confined area.

Takeoffs and *landings* should generally be made into the wind to obtain maximum airspeed with minimum groundspeed. Situations may arise which modify this general rule.

CONTENTS

Turbulence is defined as smaller masses of air moving in any direction contrary to that of the larger airmass. Barriers on the ground and the ground itself may interfere with the smooth flow of air. This interference is transmitted to upper air levels as larger, but less intense, disturbances. Therefore, the greatest turbulence usually is found at low altitudes. Gusts are sudden variations in wind velocity. Normally, gusts are dangerous only during flight at very low altitudes. The aviator may be unaware of the gust, and its cessation may reduce lift, causing the aircraft to sink or descend abruptly. Gusts cannot be planned for or anticipated. Turbulence, however, can generally be predicted. Turbulence normally exists during moderate to strong wind conditions in the following places:

☐ Near the ground on the downwind side of trees, buildings, or hills. The turbulent area is always relative in size to that of the obstacle, and relative in intensity to the velocity of the wind (fig 4-1).

FIGURE 4-1. AIR TURBULENCE (BUILDING AND TREES).

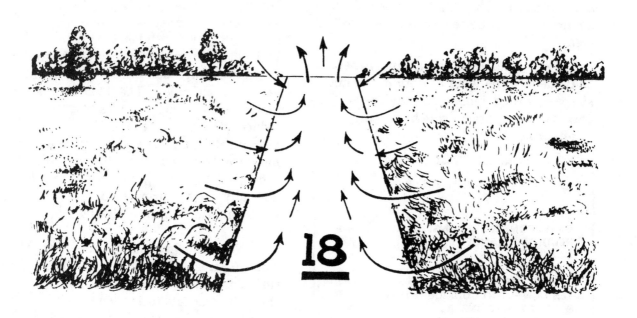

FIGURE 4-2. AIR TURBULENCE (DISSIMILAR GROUND).

☐ On the ground on the immediate upwind side of any solid barrier such as leafy trees, buildings, etc. This condition is not generally dangerous unless the wind velocity is approximately 17 knots or higher.

☐ In the air, over and slightly downwind of any sizable barrier, such as a hill. The size of the barrier and the wind velocity determine the height to which the turbulence extends.

☐ At low altitudes on bright sunny days near the border of two dissimilar types of ground, such as the edge of a ramp or runway bordered by sod (fig 4-2). This type of turbulence is caused by the upward and downward passage of heated or cooled air.

RECONNAISSANCE

A *high* and *low reconnaissance* should be conducted prior to landing in an unfamiliar area.

☐ *High Reconnaissance.* The purpose of a high reconnaissance is to determine suitability of the landing area, locate barriers and estimate their wind effect, select approach and departure axis, select a point for touchdown, and plan the flightpath for approach and takeoff. Altitude, airspeed, and flight pattern for the high reconnaissance are governed by wind and terrain features, including availability of forced landing areas. The reconnaissance should be low enough to permit study of the general area, yet not so low that attention must be divided between studying the area and avoiding obstructions to flight. It should be high enough to afford a reasonable chance of making a successful forced landing in an emergency, yet not so high that the proposed area cannot be studied adequately. A high reconnaissance is impractical during conditions that require terrain flight, because the aviator would have to climb and expose the aircraft to the threat for an unacceptable period of time.

☐ *Low Reconnaissance.*

● Except when a running landing is necessary, the low reconnaissance and approach can often be conducted together. To accomplish this, the aviator studies his approach path and the immediate vicinity of his selected touchdown point as he approaches; however, before loss of effective translational lift, or prior to descending below the barrier, he must decide whether the landing can be completed successfully. Never land in an area from which a successful takeoff cannot be made. The low reconnaissance should confirm what was learned from the high reconnaissance.

● When a running landing is contemplated because of load or high density altitude conditions, a "fly-by" type of low reconnaissance is made. Airspeed is adequate to maintain effective translational lift at an altitude sufficient to clear all obstacles and allow the aviator to concentrate on terrain features. The intended landing area should be checked for obstacles and/or obstructions in the approach path or on the landing site; and the point of intended touchdown must be selected.

● A low reconnaissance can be conducted during an approach from terrain flight; however, the landing area will normally be visible for only a very short time prior to touchdown. A longer period of time for low reconnaissance is available if a circling approach from terrain flight can be made. Aviators must evaluate the tactical situation and determine whether a circling approach will expose them to the threat.

CONFINED AREA OPERATIONS

☐ *Approach.*

●The confined area approach begins with the high reconnaissance. Plan the approach by taking into consideration several different and sometimes conflicting factors. Account for wind conditions and the best possible advantage to be obtained from them. Consider the height of barriers, and identify the lowest obstruction which would provide the best entry into the area under favorable wind conditions. Where possible, plan the flightpath to place the helicopter within reach of those areas most favorable for a forced landing. When it is not possible to keep the area in sight, specific reference points along the approach path should be selected which will keep the aviator from losing the area completely.

●Point-of-touchdown should be as far beyond the barrier as practicable to insure against the approach becoming too steep. The final stages of the approach, however, should be conducted short of downdrafts and turbulence which may be encountered at the far end of the area.

●The angle of descent should be steep enough to permit clearance of the barrier, but normally not greater than a steep approach (fig 4-3).

●Terminate the approach to the ground when surface conditions permit.

☐ *Ground Operations.* Before the helicopter is operated within the area, a ground reconnaissance should be conducted to determine suitability of the area. This reconnaissance can be made from the cockpit or by conducting a walk-around reconnaissance of the area.

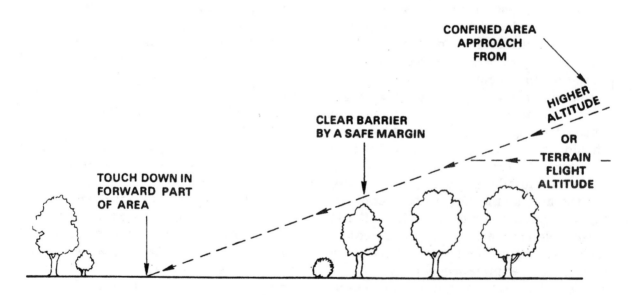

FIGURE 4-3. CONFINED AREA APPROACH AND LANDING.

☐ *Takeoff.*

● Position the helicopter for takeoff, taking advantage of wind, barriers, and anticipated forced landing areas on takeoff.

● Perform power checks and before-takeoff checks.

● Form an imaginary line from a point on the leading edge of the helicopter (e.g., gear) to the highest barrier that must be cleared. This line of ascent will be flown using only that power that is required to clear the obstacle by a safe distance (fig 4-4).

● As the barrier is cleared, the attitude of the helicopter should be adjusted to achieve a normal climb airspeed and rate of climb.

PINNACLE AND RIDGELINE OPERATIONS

A *pinnacle* is an area from which the ground drops away steeply on all sides. A *ridgeline* is a long area from which the ground drops away steeply on one or two sides, such as a bluff or precipice. The absence of pinnacle barriers does not necessarily lessen the difficulty of pinnacle operations (fig 4-5). Updrafts, downdrafts, and turbulence may still present extreme hazards. Landing areas may be small with barely enough room for a safe touchdown.

Climb to a pinnacle or ridgeline should be executed on the windward side to take advantage of updrafts (A, fig 4-5). Approach flightpath should be parallel to a ridgeline and as nearly into the wind as possible. Groundspeed during the approach is more difficult to judge because visual references are further away than during approaches over trees or flat terrain. Avoid leeward turbulence and keep the helicopter within reach of a forced landing area as long as practicable. Load, altitude, wind conditions, and terrain features determine the angle to use in the final part of the approach. If wind velocity makes crosswind landing hazardous, make a low

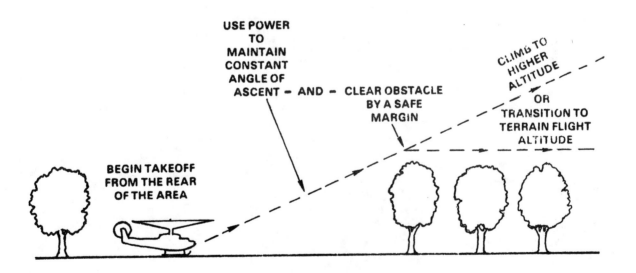

FIGURE 4-4. CONFINED AREA TAKEOFF.

coordinated turn into the wind just prior to landing.

CAUTION: Remain clear of downdrafts on the downwind side (B, fig 4-5)

Landing on a pinnacle should be made to take advantage of the long axis of the area when wind conditions permit. Touchdown should be made in the forward portion of the area and a stability check should be accomplished to insure the gear is on firm terrain that will support the weight of the helicopter safely.

Since a pinnacle is higher than immediate surrounding terrain, gaining airspeed on takeoff is more important than gaining altitude. The airspeed gained will cause a more rapid departure from the slopes of the pinnacle. In addition to covering unsafe ground quickly, a higher airspeed affords a more favorable glide angle; and thus contributes to the chances of reaching a safe area in the event of forced landing. If no suitable area is available, a higher airspeed will permit the aviator to execute a deceleration and decrease forward speed prior to autorotative landing. After clearing the pinnacle, no attempt should be made to dive the helicopter down the slope. This will result in a high rate of descent and may prevent a successful autorotative landing.

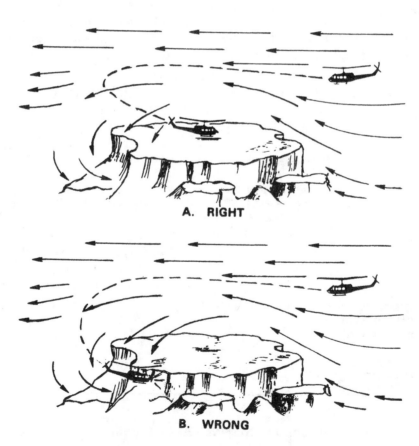

A. RIGHT

B. WRONG

FIGURE 4-5. PINNACLE APPROACH.

SLOPE OPERATIONS

☐ *General.* When a helicopter rests on a slope, the mast is perpendicular to the inclined surface, while the plane of the main rotor must parallel the true horizon or tilt slightly upslope. Thus the rotor tilts with respect to the mast. Normally, the cyclic control available for this rotor tilt is limited by cyclic control stops, static stops, mast bumping, or other mechanical limits of control travel. These control limits are reached much sooner in downslope wind conditions. Also, when the hovering helicopter hangs with one side low, there will be less control travel when landing with the low side upslope. Therefore, a slope landing site which was used once may not be acceptable with a different wind or CG helicopter loading. Also, conditions that permitted a slope landing may have changed to cause very hazardous conditions for takeoff (e.g., wind or CG loading change).

• *Approach.* The approach to a slope may not materially differ from the approach to any other landing area. However, the slope may obstruct wind passage and cause turbulence and downdrafts. Allowance must be made for wind, barriers, and forced landing sites.

● *Landing upslope or cross-slope.* If a helicopter is equipped with wheel type landing gear, brakes must be set prior to making a landing. The landing is then usually made heading upslope. With skid-type gear, slope landings should be made cross-slope. This type landing requires careful and positive control touch. The helicopter must be lowered from the true vertical by placing the uphill skid on the ground first. The downhill skid is then lowered gently to the ground. Corrective cyclic control is applied simultaneously to keep the helicopter on the landing point. The aviator must maintain positive heading control on a forward reference point and normal operating RPM until the landing is completed. To avoid mast bumping, sliding downslope, or rollover, the landing attempt should be aborted if the aviator runs out of cyclic control travel before the downhill skid is firmly on the ground.

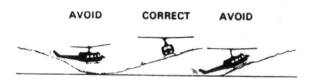

AVOID   CORRECT   AVOID

FIGURE 4-6. SLOPE OPERATIONS.

● *Landing downhill.* Landing downhill (fig 4-6) is not recommended with single main rotor type helicopters because of the possibility of striking the tail rotor on the ground.

● *Landing uphill.* If an uphill landing (fig 4-6) is necessary, landing too near the bottom of the slope may cause the tail rotor to strike the ground. In this case, and when landing downhill, the mission may sometimes be completed at a low hover.

● *Takeoff from a slope.* To lift off from a slope, the aviator moves cyclic control toward the slope and slowly adds collective pitch. The downhill skid must first be raised to place the helicopter in a level attitude before lifting it vertically to a hover.

☐ *Dynamic Rollover Characteristics.* During slope or crosswind landing and takeoff maneuvers, the helicopter is susceptible to a lateral rolling tendency called *dynamic rollover*. Each helicopter has a critical rollover angle beyond which recovery is impossible. If the critical rollover angle is exceeded, the helicopter will roll over on its side regardless of cyclic corrections introduced by the pilot. The rate of rolling motion is also critical. As the roll rate increases, it reduces the critical rollover angle at which recovery is still possible. Depending on the helicopter, the critical rollover angle may change depending on which skid or wheel is touching the ground, crosswind component, lateral offsets in center of gravity, and left pedal inputs for torque correction (single rotor systems).

● Dynamic rollover starts when the helicopter has only one skid or wheel on the ground and that gear becomes a pivot point for lateral roll (figs 4-7, 4-8). When this happens, lateral cyclic control response is more sluggish and is less effective than for the free hovering helicopter. The gear may become a pivot point for a variety of reasons, most of which are pilot induced. It may become caught on something projecting from the landing surface such as a bent piece of pierced steel planking (PSP). It could become stuck in soft asphalt or

DOWNSLOPE ROLLING MOTION

Excessive application of collective pitch in coordination with cyclic application into the slope. When the downslope skid is on the slope, excessive application of collective may result in the upslope skid rising sufficiently to exceed lateral cyclic limits and induce a downslope rolling motion.

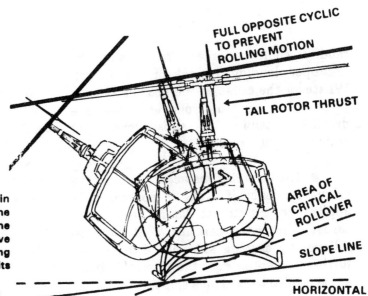

FIGURE 4-7. DOWNSLOPE ROLLING MOTION.

UPSLOPE ROLLING MOTION

Excessive application of cylic into the slope, in coordination with collective pitch application. During landings or takeoffs, this condition results in the downslope skid rising sufficiently to exceed lateral cyclic control limits and an upslope rolling motion occurs.

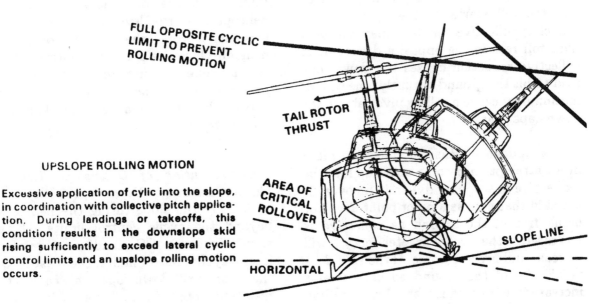

FIGURE 4-8. UPSLOPE ROLLING MOTION.

mud. It could be forced into the slope by improper landing or takeoff technique. Whatever the cause, if the gear becomes a pivot point, dynamic rollover becomes a definite possibility if subsequent pilot actions are incorrect.

● The tail rotor may contribute to the rolling tendency if cyclic is not correctly applied to counteract lateral tail rotor thrust. Crosswind can also contribute to rollover by causing sideward drift, or by further accentuating the aircraft bank angle needed to land on a slope.

● Application of collective pitch is more effective than lateral cyclic in controlling the rolling motion because it changes main rotor thrust. A smooth moderate collective pitch *reduction* may be the most effective way to stop a rolling motion. Collective must not be reduced so fast as to cause fuselage and rotor blade contact. Also, if the helicopter is on a slope and the roll starts to the upslope side, reducing collective too fast may create a high roll rate in the opposite direction. If collective reduction causes the downslope skid to hit the ground abruptly, the rate of motion may cause a roll or pivot about the downslope gear.

● Sudden increase of collective pitch in an attempt to become airborne may be ineffective in stopping dynamic rollover. If the skid that acts as a pivot point *does not* break free of the ground as collective is increased, the rollover tendency will increase and become worse. If the skid *does* break free of the ground as collective is increased, it can cause an abrupt rolling movement in the opposite direction because of pendulum effect. This movement may also become uncontrollable.

● When performing maneuvers with one skid on the ground, care must be taken to keep the helicopter trimmed, especially laterally. Control can be maintained if the pilot maintains trim, does not allow lateral roll rates to become rapid, and keeps the bank angle from exceeding the critical rollover angle for the helicopter. The pilot must fly the helicopter into the air smoothly with only small changes in pitch, roll, and yaw. Untrimmed moments must be avoided.

☐ *Prevention of Upslope Rollover During Liftoff.* Upslope rollover characteristics are possible during liftoff. Upslope rollover can result from excessive use of cyclic to hold the upslope skid against the slope. Improper use of collective pitch could then result in a rapid pivoting around the longitudinal axis of the upslope landing gear to the point of rollover. To prevent upslope rollover, the aviator should cautiously lift the downslope side of the helicopter to the level point and simultaneously work the cyclic control to neutral. Once the cyclic is neutral and/or the upslope landing gear has *no side pressure applied,* the aviator is cleared for a vertical liftoff to a hover and then to a normal takeoff.

☐ *Prevention of Downslope Rollover During Landing.* Downslope rollover is caused by the slope tilting the helicopter beyond the cyclic control limits. If the slope (wind or CG conditions) exceeds lateral cyclic control limits, the mast forces the rotor to tilt downslope. This causes the resultant rotor lift to have a downslope component, even with full upslope cyclic applied. To prevent downslope rollover during landing, the aviator should slowly descend vertically to a light ground contact with the upslope skid. While observing lateral level reference frames, he should pause while checking positive heading control. Then using careful collective pitch control, he should slowly and cautiously lower the downslope skid. As the cyclic stick nears the lateral stop, he should pause to compare the distance to go with the lateral control travel remaining. (See limits in appropriate Operator's Manual.) If it appears that the cyclic will contact the upslope control stop before the downslope skid is firmly on the ground, he should return the helicopter to a level attitude and abort the slope landing. He should then lift off and move a few feet for another attempt on a lesser slope.

☐ *Prevention of Downslope Rollover During Liftoff.* If a landing was inadvertently completed on an excessive slope, and during an attempt to liftoff the upslope skid tends to rise, the aviator should smoothly lower the collective pitch. The problem is that with full cyclic applied, the resultant lift of the main rotor is not vertical or directed upslope sufficiently to raise the downslope skid. Therefore, if the upslope skid raises, the mast causes the resultant rotor lift to move further downslope. This increases the downslope roll tendency which increases with added collective pitch. The corrective action is to reduce power at the first sign of lateral roll around the downslope skid. Before further liftoff attempts are made, appropriate aviator action may be to:

● Await different wind conditions.

● Change CG loading.

● Dig out under the upslope gear.

● Notify operations to send a recovery crew.

GENERAL PRECAUTIONS

Certain general rules apply to operations in any type of confined area, slope, or pinnacle. Some of the more important of these rules are:

☐ Know wind direction and approximate velocity at all times. Plan landings and takeoffs with this knowledge in mind.

☐ Plan the flightpath, both for approach and takeoff, to take maximum advantage of forced-landing areas.

☐ Operate the helicopter as near to its normal capabilities as the situation allows. The angle of descent should be no steeper than that necessary to clear existing barriers and to land on a preselected spot. Angle of climb in takeoff should be no steeper than that necessary to clear all barriers in the takeoff path.

☐ If low hovering is not made hazardous by the terrrain, to minimize the effect of turbulence and to conserve power, the helicopter should be hovered at a lower altitude than normal when in a confined area. High grass or weeds will decrease efficiency of the ground effect; but hovering low or taking off from the ground will partially compensate for this loss of ground effect.

☐ Make every landing to a specific point, not merely into a general area. The more confined the area, the more essential that the helicopter be landed precisely upon a definite point. The landing point must be kept in sight during the final approach, particularly during the more critical final phase.

☐ Consideration should be given to increases in terrain elevation between the point of original takeoff and subsequent areas of operation.

☐ Brakes (on wheeled helicopters) should be set prior to initiating the approach for a confined area landing, except for a running landing or when the landing area is known to be level. This precaution precludes unexpected roll after touchdown. A slope landing almost invariably results in a wheel roll unless the brakes are preset.

☐ In entering any restricted area, judge the diameter clearance of main rotor blades; but remain especially alert to prevent possible damage to the tail rotor. Not only must the angle of descent over a barrier clear the tail rotor of all obstructions, but caution must be exercised on the ground to avoid swinging the tail rotor into trees, boulders, or other objects. The aviator is responsible to see that personnel remain clear of the tail rotor at all times.

CHAPTER 5

PRECAUTIONARY MEASURES
AND CRITICAL CONDITIONS

GENERAL PRECAUTIONARY RULES

Because of its unique flight characteristics, a helicopter is capable of many missions no other aircraft can perform. A rotary-wing aviator must, however, realize the hazards involved in helicopter flight. He should know how to apply precautions which might save the helicopter or even his life. He should:

☐ Check weight and balance prior to flying.

CONTENTS

☐ Assure that any object placed in the cockpit of a helicopter is well secured to prevent fouling of the controls.

☐ Caution approaching or departing passengers of main rotor/tail rotor dangers at all times during ground operations. Personnel carrying long objects such as pipe, wood, tripods, etc., should not be allowed to approach a helicopter whose rotor blades are turning, because of the danger of these objects striking the rotor blades.

☐ Ground taxi slowly.

☐ Maintain normal operating rotor RPM during all flight conditions.

☐ Hover for a moment before beginning forward flight.

☐ Avoid high hovering and become familiar with the height velocity diagram in the operator's handbook.

☐ Use caution when hovering on the lee side of buildings or obstructions.

☐ Avoid hovering in dusty areas or debris-covered areas.

☐ Develop and use a constant cross-check for engine, transmission, and systems instruments.

☐ Perform only maneuvers authorized in the Operator's Manual.

☐ When flying in rough, gusty air, maintain penetration airspeed recommended in the aircraft Operator's Manual.

☐ Always clear the area overhead, ahead, to each side, and below, before entering practice autorotations.

☐ Avoid engine and rotor overspeeding beyond the Operator's Manual recommendations.

ROTOR RPM OPERATING LIMITS

Limits of rotor RPM vary with each type of helicopter. In general:

☐ *Low rotor RPM limits* are determined to prevent high blade coning and excessive flapping angles. In engine failure autorotation, rotor RPM decay below certain levels will not respond to corrective measures. Below safe normal rotor RPM limits, there is:

• Greater danger of mast bumping or of the rotor blades striking the fuselage.

• Possible sluggish control response.

☐ *High rotor RPM limits* are established to prevent possible structural failure and damage to rotating assemblies caused by too high centrifugal loads developed by the rotor blades.

TURBINE ENGINE OPERATING LIMITATIONS

The gas turbine is a most reliable and trouble-free engine. It operates in a continuous cycle which is conducive to long engine life. The engine is designed to operate at high power outputs and operates most efficiently at high powers. However, the operating limitations of the engine must be observed meticulously if the engine is to exhibit the long, trouble-free life which is expected of it.

☐ *Exhaust gas temperature* provides one of the most important limitations upon the operation of the gas turbine. The exhaust gas temperature may be taken at any of a number of positions following the final turbine stage in the engine. It is for this reason that it is difficult to compare temperatures between models. When the turbine is designed, an instrumented engine is used to determine the proper position to take the exhaust gas temperature so the most reliable indication of turbine temperature is obtained. It is the *turbine temperature* which is of importance and is the true limitation. It is the turbine which puts the lid on the whole engine with its limiting temperature, caused by the material of which it is constructed and the stresses on the material caused by the aerodynamic and centrifugal loads. The exhaust gas temperature is not a direct reading of the limitation, but an indirect reading. However, the limitations so indicated must be carefully obeyed.

☐ In conjunction with the exhaust gas temperature, *an RPM limitation* will be established on the engine. The RPM limitation is primarily a stress limitation and is caused by the maximum stress which the turbine can withstand at the operating temperatures. It is for this reason that the temperature and RPM limitations go together and are listed in the pilot's handbook as a dual limitation.

☐ Of course, an overspeed engine condition breeds overtemperature. In this relation they tend to go together. However, an overtemperature may occur without overspeed, such as during an improper start. The overtemperature and overspeed limitations which are listed together in the pilot's handbook usually provide *starting temperature* limitations.

☐ The turbine is under two distinct types of *structural stress*. It is undergoing *creep*, that elastic phenomenon caused by stress at high temperatures. It is also subject to *fatigue* due to the high frequency aerodynamic and structural vibrations which occur in the engine. Both of these effects are cumulative.

● If the temperature is elevated for a period of time, the rate of *creep* will increase. If simultaneously the stress is increased, the rate of creep will increase by an order of magnitude. Therefore, while damage may not be visible to the eye following an overstress and/or overtemperature, there will be some shortening of engine life. It is therefore imperative that there be some recording of the limitation which was exceeded, so that a judgment may be made as to when the engine must be inspected for creep damage.

● A similar situation exists with respect to *fatigue* damage. An overspeed condition accompanied by overtemperature will increase the fatigue environment to the point that significant increases in the fatigue damage may occur.

● A gross overstress or overtemperature of the turbine section will produce damage that is apparent to the eye. However, *creep* and *fatigue* damage accumulated through periods of small overstress and overtemperature will cause damage which will shorten the service life and may cause failure to occur prior to the normal removal and inspection dates.

The magnitude of the overstress produced by the overspeed is not proportional to the overspeed, but increases somewhat more rapidly than the overspeed. Therefore a 5-percent overspeed in RPM will produce approximately a 10-percent overstress. This large increase in stress with RPM not only shortens the life of the turbine, but has adverse effects on the compressor and other components of the turbine which may be sensitive to vibration and fatigue.

It is well, therefore, for the pilot to be aware of the various combinations of RPM and temperatures which are allowable for certain periods of time. These limitations may be listed in blocks, some of which may be allowed, some of which must be reported, some of which require engine removal and inspection, and some of which require an engine change. Although it is embarrassing for the pilot to make such a report, particularly when no damage is visible, it is most important that he do so if the proper safety measures are to be taken.

EXTREME ATTITUDES AND OVERCONTROLLING

Extreme attitudes and overcontrolling should be avoided. See approved maneuvers in the Operator's Manual.

☐ A helicopter should not be loaded so as to cause an extreme tail-low attitude.

☐ Heavy loading foward of the center of gravity should be avoided. Limited aft travel of the cyclic stick results, endangering controllability.

☐ Extreme nose-low attitude should be avoided when executing a takeoff. Such an attitude may require more power than the engine can deliver and will allow the helicopter to settle to the ground in an unsafe landing attitude. In the event of power loss on takeoff, a comparatively level attitude can assure a safe touchdown.

☐ Rearward cyclic control should never be abruptly applied. The violent backward-pitching action of the rotor disk may cause the main rotor blades to flex downward into the airframe.

☐ Large or unnecessary movements of the cyclic control should be avoided while at a hover. Such movements of the cyclic control can cause sufficient loss of lift, under certain conditions, to make the helicopter inadvertently settle to the ground.

☐ When executing 360° hovering turns in winds of 10 knots or more, the tail of the helicopter will rise when the downwind portion of the turn is reached. When this happens, if the rear cyclic control limit is exceeded, the helicopter will accelerate forward; and a landing must be made immediately.

☐ Avoid abrupt antitorque pedal movements while at a hover. Turns in excess of 360° in 15 seconds will place stress on the tail boom that may result in a failure.

HIGH SPEED AUTOROTATIONS

When entering autorotations in most helicopters at high airspeeds, the nose pitches upward after collective pitch is lowered. With an aft center of gravity, this condition can become critical by having insufficient forward cyclic control to effect a recovery. (A large amount of forward cyclic control is used even in recovery of a well-balanced helicopter.) When the nose pitches up, application of forward cyclic may cause mast bumping. To avoid this unsafe condition, a nose-high attitude should be maintained. This deceleration attitude will slow the helicopter. Depending on the airspeed of the helicopter, additional aft cyclic may be required. Upon decelerating to the desired autorotational airspeed, the attitude of the helicopter is readjusted to maintain normal descent airspeed. Upon entering the deceleration attitude, the collective is lowered to maintain normal operating RPM. At high airspeeds, it may be necessary to maintain pitch in the blades to control the RPM. As the helicopter decelerates to the best glide airspeed, the pitch should be in the full down position.

OPERATIONS WITH REDUCED VISIBILITY & LOW CEILING CONDITIONS

By reducing speed to the limits of visibility so that a rapid deceleration may be executed if an obstacle appears in the flightpath, flight can be continued with low ceilings and visibility. The aviator must, however, be aware of the hazards of downwind flight at low altitudes under these conditions. Whenever further flight appears hazardous, an aviator can execute a landing (vertical if necessary) and remain on the ground until further flight is possible.

OPERATIONS IN PRECIPITATION

☐ *Rain and Snow.* Light rain and snow have comparatively little effect on the helicopter, and flight can usually be continued. However, heavy rain and snow have an abrasive effect on the rotor blades; therefore, flight should be discontinued during heavy rain or snow.

☐ *Hail.* Hail, the most serious type of precipitation from an abrasive standpoint, should be avoided by skirting weather areas where hail is likely. If hail is encountered during flight, a landing should be made as soon as possible and the helicopter inspected for damage.

☐ *Freezing Rain.* Freezing rain is the most dangerous type of precipitation encountered. Ice quickly forms on the windshield, and complete loss of vision through the windshield can be expected as the ice thickens. By looking to the side or jettisoning the door, the aviator may retain enough visibility to effect a safe landing.

WARNING: An aviator should never stare through a windshield on which ice is forming; a loss of sense of direction and movement result.

Formation of ice on the rotor blades causes an unbalanced condition and a disruption of streamlined airflow. The resultant loss of airfoil symmetry may cause the center of pressure to move as the angle of attack changes, resulting in reduced control effect and unusual feedback of undesirable control pressures. Uneven ice formation causes unbalanced rotor blades which produce excessive vibration of the entire helicopter.

CAUTION: The aviator must not attempt to throw ice off the blades by sudden rotor acceleration, or by rapid control movements. At best, only a small portion of the blade ice could be thrown off, probably incurring additional rotor unbalance.

Under weather conditions in which temperature and dewpoint are close together and near freezing, ice may build up rapidly on a rotor system operating at low RPM (as in a parked helicopter with idling engine). When these conditions are suspected, the aviator should stop the engine and inspect the rotor blades before attempting a takeoff.

Additional indications of icing include:

● Ice forming on the windshield.

● Loss of RPM. As the ice builds up, drag increases, causing a loss in RPM. The aviator must repeatedly add power and/or reduce pitch to maintain RPM.

● Mushy cyclic control.

● Excessive vibration.

CAUTION: When this condition occurs, it may not be possible to maintain an autorotational speed above the lower limit.

AIR DENSITY AND PRESSURE ALTITUDE

Low air density at high pressure altitude reduces helicopter efficiency during hot weather operation. When air is subjected to heat, it expands and becomes thinner (fewer air particles per cubic foot). Since lift is obtained from air particles and since, under thinner air conditions, there are fewer air particles per cubic foot, it is necessary to operate the rotor blades at a higher angle of attack. This condition requires more power and reduces the load-carrying capability of the helicopter. Normal ascent, hovering, and descent may become impossible; running takeoffs and landings may become necessary as operation becomes more critical.

FLIGHT TECHNIQUE IN HOT WEATHER

When flying in hot weather, the aviator should:

☐ Make full use of wind and translational lift.

☐ Hover as low as possible and no longer than necessary.

☐ Maintain maximum allowable engine RPM.

☐ Accelerate very slowly into forward flight.

☐ Employ running takeoffs and landings when necessary.

☐ Use caution in maximum performance takeoffs and steep approaches. Complete a power check prior to takeoff.

☐ Avoid high rates of descent in all approaches.

OTHER OPERATIONS

☐ *High-Altitude Operation.* Although civil and military tests have proved that the helicopter is capable of performing successfully at high altitudes, they have also proved that high-altitude operation usually is marginal and demands a high degree of aviator proficiency. Aviators assigned high-altitude missions must be thoroughly familiar with the factors affecting helicopter performance and the flight techniques involved. To operate successfully at high altitudes, the aviator must first determine that the factors affecting helicopter performance do not exceed the operating limits of the machine. The three major factors to understand are:

① *Air density.*

● An increase in altitude causes a decrease in air density.

● An increase in temperature causes a decrease in air density.

● An increase in humidity causes a decrease in air density.

② *Wind.*

● If there is sufficient wind velocity to afford translational lift while hovering, helicopter performance is improved considerably.

● Translational lift, present with any forward speed or headwind, has an insignificant effect until speeds of approximately 15 to 20 knots are obtained.

③ *Load.*

● Load is a variable factor and must be considered carefully by the aviator. Smaller amounts of fuel may be carried to improve performance or increase useful load; however, this necessitates a sacrifice in range.

● Under conditions of high density altitude, additional engine power is required to compensate for the thin air. If the maximum gross weight of the helicopter exceeds the limits of available engine power, a reduction in load may be necessary.

● Due to changes of density altitude and wind velocity during the day, the weight-carrying capability of a particular helicopter may vary many times during a single day.

● Established service ceilings for each helicopter must be considered in computing maximum load for safe operations.

☐ *Effect of Altitude on Instrument Readings.* The thinner air of higher altitudes causes the airspeed indicator to read low. True airspeed may be roughly computed by adding 2 percent to the indicated airspeed for each 1,000 feet of altitude above sea level. For example, an indicated airspeed of 100 knots at 10,000 feet will be a true airspeed of 120 knots. A more accurate computation may be made by using the dead-reckoning navigational computer.

☐ *Effect of Altitude on Engine Power.* Engine power is reduced as air density decreases. Figure 10-1 shows a typical plot of turbine engine power versus density altitude. See the appropriate aircraft Operator's Manual for specific performance charts for each aircraft.

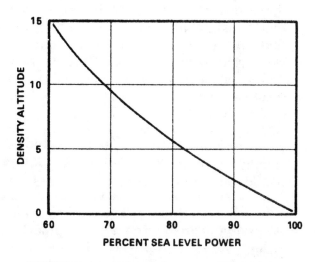

FIGURE 10-1. TURBINE ENGINE POWER OUTPUT VERSUS DENSITY ALTITUDE

□ *High Altitude Flight Techniques*. Of the three major factors limiting helicopter performance at high altitude, only load may be controlled by the aviator. At the expense of range, smaller amounts of fuel may be carried to improve performance or increase useful load. The weight and balance aircraft records should be consulted to insure efficient loading. Where practical, running landings and takeoffs could be used. Favorable wind conditions are helpful, with landings and takeoffs directly into the wind if possible. In mountainous terrain, flight should be on the upwind side of slopes to take advantage of updrafts. When landing on ridges, the safest approach is usually made lengthwise of the ridge, flying near the upwind edge to avoid possible downdrafts and to be in position to autorotate down the upwind side of the slope in case of forced landing. Using the updraft in this manner results in lower rate of descent, improved glide ratio, and greater choice of a landing area.

□ *Operations Over Tall Grass*. Tall grass disrupts airflow and disturbs normal downwash angle with two results: the induced rotor drag is increased and the rotor airflow pattern is changed. More power will be required to hover, and takeoff may be very difficult.

□ *Operations Over Water*. Altitude is difficult to determine when operating over water with a smooth or glassy surface. Thus, caution must be exercised to prevent the helicopter from inadvertently striking the water or from terminating approach at a high hover. This problem does not exist over rough water, but a very rough water surface may disperse the "ground" effect and thereby require more power to hover.

Movements of the water surface, wind ripples, waves, current flow, or even agitation by the helicopter's own rotorwash tend to give the aviator a false feeling of helicopter movement. The aviator should avoid staring at the water; he can remain oriented by frequent reference to objects in the water such as ships, buoys, floating debris, or objects on a distant shoreline.

MAST BUMPING IN THE SEMIRIGID ROTOR SYSTEM

Inappropriate pilot response to low-G maneuvers, engine failure, and some types of tail rotor failure, can lead to mast bumping and possible rotor mast failure. Mast bumping is the result of excessive rotor flapping. Each rotor system design has a maximum flapping angle at which a static stop prevents further flapping. If flapping exceeds the design value the static stop contacts the mast. It is the violent contact between the static stop and the mast during flight that causes mast damage or separation. This contact must be avoided at all costs.

Mast bumping is directly related to how much the pilot allows the blade system to flap. In straight-and-level flight, blade flapping is minimal—perhaps 2 degrees under usual flight conditions. Flapping angles increase moderately with high forward speeds, at low rotor RPM, at high density altitudes, at high gross weights, and during turbulence. Aircraft maneuvering, such as sideslips or low-speed flight at extreme CG positions, can induce larger flapping angles.

☐ Excessive flapping is most probable when pilots allow the aircraft to approach *low-G conditions*. Common maneuvers leading to low-G conditions include crossing a ridgeline during high speed terrain flight, masking and unmasking, acquiring or staying on a target, and recovery from a pullup. Each of these maneuvers has in common an application of forward cyclic or a reduction of collective pitch that unloads the main rotor. The combinations of down collective and forward cyclic that produce low-Gs essentially cancel the lift; and therefore thrust, produced by the main rotor. Absence of main rotor thrust makes lateral cyclic control ineffective, so lateral cyclic movement produces no change of fuselage attitude. The aircraft does not respond to lateral cyclic because the pilot gave up G loading on the rotor disk when the maneuver was initiated.

● Figure 10-2 illustrates what happens during the low-G condition. In sketch A, the helicopter rotor is loaded and all forces are in balance as in normal cruise or a steady state cyclic climb.

● Sketch B shows the helicopter in a low-G condition produced by an abrupt pilot input of forward cyclic. Note that the main rotor is unloaded; that is, thrust is reduced significantly. The aircraft is rolling to the right because tail rotor thrust is no longer offset by the main rotor thrust. Forces are not in balance because the pilot gave up rotor disk loading when the zero-G maneuver was initiated.

● Sketch C shows what happens when the pilot applies left lateral cyclic to counter the right roll. This is a normal pilot reaction to correct for a right roll; but, in this case, it is an incorrect reaction.

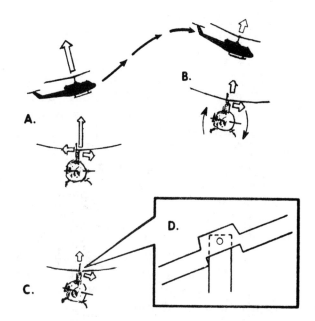

FIGURE 10-2. ZERO-G MANEUVER

RESULTING IN MAST BUMPING.

Because the rotor is unloaded, the fuselage does not follow the rotor disk and severe flapping results. The maximum design flapping angle is exceeded and **mast bumping** occurs as shown in sketch D.

● How should the pilot recover from the noseover maneuver which caused the low-G condition? Of course, the best method is to avoid the low-G condition by using more gradual forward cyclic. The **rate and extent** of cyclic motion should be adjusted to keep the rotor loaded at **all times**. Mast bumping is minimized by staying above ½ G at all times, thereby preventing the low-G condition and tendency to roll right. However, if the rotor becomes unloaded during a low-G maneuver, it is absolutely essential to recover rotor thrust by *smoothly applying aft cyclic*. Once rotor thrust is restored, then left cyclic will be effective in rolling the aircraft to a level flight attitude.

☐ Another possible cause of mast bumping is *engine failure*. If the pilot responds correctly to an engine failure, mast bumping will not occur. However, an incorrect pilot reaction could cause mast bumping.

• Assume the helicopter is flying in a normal cruise attitude. The longitudinal axis, and therefore the nose, is pitched down slightly and the rotor disk is tilted slightly forward. Viewed from the rear, the rotor disk is tilted slightly to the left to counter the tail rotor thrust to the right. The roll axis is located below the tail rotor thrust axis. From above, the main rotor is turning counterclockwise. Torque produces a clockwise force on the fuselage which is counteracted by tail rotor thrust to the right. All forces are balanced and the helicopter is in equilibrium.

• When the engine stops, the rotor RPM and airspeed begin to decay with some loss of altitude. Because the engine is no longer driving the main rotor and RPM is decreasing, the torque about the mast is diminishing. The tail rotor continues to thrust to the right causing the aircraft nose to yaw left. Tail rotor thrust is above the longitudinal axis and initiates fuselage roll to the right. Left yaw exposes the right side of the fuselage to the relative wind which aggravates the roll to the right.

• The pilot sees an abrupt change in aircraft attitude. The nose is down and yaws left. The aircraft appears to be in a roll to the right. Normal pilot reaction is to apply right pedal and left aft cyclic. Left aft cyclic immediately tilts the rotor disk left and aft which results in larger flapping angles and possible mast bumping. The pilot has reacted to the symptom and not the primary problem. The symptom is the roll...the problem is power loss. The correct remedy is to lower collective pitch to maintain rotor RPM and apply right pedal to trim the aircraft. Avoid abrupt or very large cyclic corrections until the rotor RPM is back in the normal range.

☐ A third possible cause of mast bumping is tail *rotor failure*. In the description that follows, assume that the failure causes tail rotor thrust to go to zero and only the tail fin remains to resist torque about the main rotor mast.

• At the instant of tail rotor failure, when antitorque thrust goes to zero, the aircraft yaws right and rolls left. The yaw attitude exposes the left side and nose of the aircraft to the relative wind which contributes to left roll and a nose-down attitude. Absence of tail rotor thrust also aggravates the tendency to roll left.

• The pilot sees an abrupt right yaw, left roll and nose-down attitude. Normal pilot reaction is to move the cyclic aft right and apply left pedal. With the fuselage already rolling left, right cyclic tilts the rotor disk right toward the fuselage and drastically increases blade flapping. Mast bumping becomes a possibility. The pilot has reacted to the symptom and not the primary problem. The symptom is the nose low, and roll left...the problem is torque tending to yaw the aircraft. Correct pilot reaction for this failure is immediate reduction in power to reduce torque. This will reduce the yaw, allowing time to correct for the roll tendency. With reduced throttle and collective, keep airspeed slightly above the normal autorotative glide speed. Experiment with gentle throttle and pitch application to see if some degree of powered flight can be resumed.

REMEMBER

The single most important message regarding all types of mast bumping is that the pilot can prevent mast bumping by the way the aircraft is handled. Control inputs must be smooth and gradual even in different situations such as low-G situation. It is the abrupt, full range pilot control inputs combined with low-G conditions, engine failure, or tail rotor failure that cause mast bumping.